CHRISTIAN ETHICS

By

J. OSCAR BASS, PhD

© 2003, 2004 by J. Oscar Bass, PhD. All rights reserved.

No part of this book may be reproduced, stored in a retrieval system, or transmitted by any means, electronic, mechanical, photocopying, recording, or otherwise, without written permission from the author.

ISBN: 1-4140-4158-6 (e-book)
ISBN: 1-4140-4157-8 (Paperback)

This book is printed on acid free paper.

1stBooks - rev. 11/17/03

ACKNOWLEDGEMENTS

I am uniquely blessed to count with the wholehearted support of so many people near and dear to me to whom I desire to express my most sincere gratitude and recognition.

To my family, for their unwavering love, affection and support.

To God for giving me life and to Jesus Christ who is my supreme example of ethicality and provider of the gifts to do His work, including writing this book.

To my literary editor, Sylvia Edwards Davis, who shared my vision, caught my enthusiasm and guided me through the writing process.

To Mary Wells, Executive Director and CEO of Family Service of Burlington County, who stood by me when others turned away and invited me to be an agency Chaplain and to serve on the Ethics Committee for that large agency where I could practice ethicality from a non-sectarian point of view.

To Valaiporn Viriyakovint, my Thai colleague in Bangkok, who opened venues where I could teach Ethics in a predominantly Buddhist culture and thus strengthened my resolve to stay the course.

INTRODUCTION

You are a reader living in the third millennium. As such, you have access to almost every word ever written, the Internet, the media. You are an infinitely more aware and savvy reader than, say, a reader three centuries ago. Your life occurs at a more accelerated pace. Technology and science bring so much information, so relentlessly, that you can hardly assimilate it fast enough. As a reader you therefore present an interesting challenge. I need to find a language through which I can communicate with you as directly and effectively as possible, but without distorting the sacred nature of the eternal teachings of Jesus. Words will have to transmit truths that exist outside the intellectual realm of thought. They exist in the world of the spirit. And yet, in order for me to offer you the key to this wisdom, I must appeal to your intellect. Hopefully, after assimilating and thinking about these ideas, you will be able to translate their wisdom from the language of your mind into the language of your spirit.

No matter how sophisticated we become, and how well we learn to control and improve our material and intellectual circumstances, we cannot help but live in a world of opposites. We must travel through darkness and light, life and death, despair and joy. Every day we must make decisions that will have an impact on the lives of others. For half a century I have counseled people, both Christian and Non-Christian, who agonized in emotional pain and frustration because they were not sure how to respond to situations of right and wrong confronting them. Through the years, as I met more and more people, I started to recognize common threads in their dilemmas. I came to the realization that these ethical journeys are in essence very similar to the experience of the human condition in any century.

The image that comes to mind is that of a labyrinth, with a starting point of despair and a desired final destination of joy. We are all in the labyrinth, trying to find our way to joy. I am reminded of a story that my editor related to me. She once had the opportunity to visit Hampton Court, the enchanting palace built by King Henry VIII in England. Her uncle showed her around and led her to one of the landmarks of the place: a huge garden maze elaborately built of intersecting eight-foot high hedges. As she was about to enter, her uncle whispered in her ear, "just keep your right hand touching the wall and never let go - you will find the way out". She followed the advice and, sure enough, found her way out effortlessly. As she emerged she looked at the other people still fumbling through the twists and turns and she asked her amused uncle, "How come everybody else doesn't know about this?" This is the way I feel about the teachings of Jesus. It is the goal of this book to whisper in your ear that there is a way out, and that it is available to anybody who will listen. The problems that we encounter today in our contemporary discussion of ethics are different than those in the past, but the way out of the labyrinth is the same. I am hereby extending an invitation to you. It is the same invitation that I received many years ago, and decided to accept. It is the invitation that changed my life forever. I am inviting you to travel from despair into joy by following our leader, Jesus Christ. We are fortunate to not only have His words, but also his example to learn from. He lived as one of us, and experienced the full spectrum or our life experience. Jesus is the way out of the labyrinth. His guiding principles will show you the way from darkness into light.

In our discussion of Christian Ethics, I have chosen topics that are common to all of us. I categorize these topics into two main areas. I discuss topics in our inner circle, such as our relationships with our parents, our spouses, and our work. I also discuss topics in the wider circle of our experience, such as politics, war and the media. For the illustration of this discussion I have chosen a variety of examples - from water-cooler gossip all the way to the media coverage of a potential impeachment of a President. (I would like to point out that in most of my examples, for the sake of brevity, I refer to the masculine gender as including both male and female).

I am confident that you will find the discussion vivid, contemporary and helpful, whatever your religious beliefs might be. This book aims to provide a roadmap, a sort of compass, that you can use to guide your ethical decisions. I would consider this book a success if it serves to remind you that at every twist and turn of your personal labyrinth, all you need to do is turn your heart towards Jesus. His wisdom is always there, just waiting for you, as soon as you are willing to listen.

TABLE OF CONTENTS

1. The Precursors of Christian Ethics

"Look beneath the surface; let not the several quality
of a thing nor its worth escape thee."
Marcus Aurelius Antoninus

Have you ever wondered what the Easter Bunny has to do with the Passion and Resurrection of Our Lord Jesus Christ? You are certainly not alone. During Christmas, your bewilderment might grow to an extreme, considering the daunting array of characters with glowing-red-noses or jingling bells that urge us to shop, decorate, eat, drink and be merry. Poor Baby Jesus away in his manger keeps getting pushed further and further into the background. Setting aside for a moment the obvious commercial opportunity provided by millions of wide-eyed children waiting for Santa and millions of parents dutifully pulling out their credit cards, it occurs to me that these traditions offer a simple way to transmit an idea from one generation to the next. Looking at this folklore in a benign light, we can find in them a tool to familiarize a small child with the joy of Christmas before he is able to grasp its true meaning. The child will feel the joy of small miracles in preparation to understand the great miracle of Jesus. Hopefully, with time, as the child matures, the true significance of the remembrance will replace the fluff. The spirit of giving will replace the spirit of getting. The adult, as he becomes able to recognize the gift that God gave to us through the birth of Jesus, will evoke the joy that he felt as a child. In turn, this adult, as a parent will probably transmit these values to the next generation through similar means, stuffing stockings and decking the halls with boughs of holly. This parent will resort to the popular metaphor of the gifts and the decorations to mark the occasion as a special time of year in terms that the young child can understand. The use of myth to transmit core values and principles has been a constant throughout antiquity, both in a secular and a religious framework.

In our study of Christian Ethics we are concerned with the eternal and unbending teachings of Jesus Christ, as applied to us believers in every aspect of our lives. But we must not forget that the world did not begin with the birth of our Lord. So what about Ethics before the arrival of Jesus Christ? Were there no guiding principles to rule the moral behavior of men back in those days? In all fairness, we must admit that the teachings that we follow as Christians stem from a very thin slice in the history of mankind: the three short years of the active life of Jesus. Furthermore, all our guidance comes from the accounts of his life described by his disciples, some of whom scarcely knew how to read and write. Even worse, the apostles were sent out into the world to spread these teachings to crowds of peasants, slaves, illiterate and poor people, who in turn set out to carry the message to other people and places. And yet these profound truths were such that they multiplied and gave spiritual life to millions, and became the guiding light that present-day Christians are so fortunate to have. The Christian Church underwent many transformations and influences, some of them less than pious. But through the centuries, though the professors of the faith were imperfect and flawed, the doctrine and real life example of Jesus was the unfailing source of spiritual fortitude that raised Christianity to the highest standards of moral virtue. Amid all the stumblings and failings, fanaticism and persecution, the Church could always fall back to the essential character of Jesus and His teachings not only in theory but in His actions during His time on earth.

The Bible of the earliest Christians was identical with the Hebrew scriptures of the Jewish communities. Whenever Jesus or the writers of the New Testament refer to the scriptures, they mean the canon of Torah, Prophets, and Writings that Jews regarded as divinely inspired, written under the direct dictation of God. In Jewish tradition, Rabbis search the Holy Text of the Torah, the Law of God, for clues to authoritative rules for living, or to interpret the meaning of the ancient text in the context of the present circumstances. Christian sacraments that we are familiar with, such as Baptism and Communion (a common meal) trace their theological origin to the Old Testament. In Galatians 4:21-26 Paul refers to the Old Testament story of Sarah and Hagar with the qualification that it must be interpreted allegorically; meaning that the text carries a deeper meaning that what its words seem to suggest.

The interpretation of an authoritative text as having a deeper meaning was an old practice among the Greeks, as in the interpretation of Homer and the early poets. The stories are not to be taken literally but figuratively, interpreted as extended and elaborate metaphors. These metaphors are contrived to make visible that which we cannot otherwise see. In this way, since the beginning of time, principles and ideas were transmitted through myth. Our ancestors may have told stories of animals and hunting prowess, so as to develop these survival skills in their young. Fairy tales many times represent the triumph of virtue over evil. In every myth there is likely to be a hero, who makes a journey throughout daunting obstacles to overcome them and reach success. The mythical hero reminds us of our own struggles to overcome our dark passions, our fallible human nature. We carry these stories in our minds. Even if we don't remember the exact details of the story of Narcissus, the notion stays with us that an excess of self-devotion will lead us to ruin. Then, as the situation arises in our lives, we have a point of reference that helps put our own experience in perspective, like a map that we carry in our pocket and only need to pull out when we come to a fork in the road. Myths take many shapes and vary widely between different cultures, and yet comparable stories can be found in divergent traditions. This may be because the human experience transcends time or space, and metaphors signify the ultimate reality that lies beneath the surface, to call us to a deeper awareness. If we have the opportunity to read Plato, Aristotle, or the teachings of ancient religions such as Buddhism, Hinduism, Judaism, Confucianism, among others, we will recognize many of the eternal values that Jesus made flesh through His life. Ideals such as the service to those who suffer are widely accepted as desirable and worthy.

Christian ethics are unquestionably religious; any attempt to abstract them from their spiritual content would distort the teachings. There is no set of rules that we can refer to when faced with concrete questions of moral conduct and character. Rather, they provide an account of God's will and the work and teachings and ultimate sacrifice of His loving Son, Jesus. Trying to force Christian Ethics into a systematic list would impoverish the teachings and rob them of their profound mystery.

2. What is Christian Ethics?

By definition, ethics is the discipline dealing with what is good and bad, and with moral duty and obligation. It is a set of principles or values. It is a guiding philosophy that affects our behavior. Unlike the laws of nature, in human behavior we have a choice. Water exposed to temperatures under 32 degrees Farenheit at sea level will freeze. It will do this every time, without variation, water doesn't choose to freeze, it just does. In our lives, we have a choice regarding our behavior, and choices bring with them their own set of complications.

As we make our transition from childhood into adulthood, we push the distinct set of rules imposed by our parents to the background, and we face our own particular set of choices. We have now more access to information than ever before, to the extent that it staggers our imagination. In the resulting clutter, the right decision is not clearly discernible from the wrong one. Just like stepping into a still, clean pond, we feel confident that we will safely find our footing. As soon as we get in, we disturb the bottom and cause ripples on the surface, and we can't see clearly anymore. We loose our initial confidence and we are not quite sure of the next step. It is in our basic human dignity to seek the right course of action, at every step, in harmony with our social setting but without abdication of our character. We need guiding principles to be able to tell right from wrong. We can't tell if something is good or bad unless we have some standard to compare it to. In order to tell if a wall is leaning, we must first have an idea of what a straight wall looks like. The aim of this book is to provide a helpful guide on where and how to find such direction.

Think of ethics as a common language. We assign sounds to a combination of letters. In this way, when I write a recipe and ask for "milk" and you read it, we can both be reasonably sure that we are referring to the same ingredient. Supposing that we each assigned our own interpretation to every word, we would not be able to understand each other, and we would eventually give up any attempt at communication. Chaos would ensue. In the same way, ethics as a guiding philosophy is the language that allows us to recognize the basic underlying values and interact with each other in a meaningful way. It is important to note that the substance "milk" itself remains the same; regardless of the word we use to describe it. It does not change according to our description of it, or to how we would wish it to be. In the same way, moral principles are universal, unchanging and inflexible. They are not open to our own preferences or interpretation. It does not matter if a particular course of action is not convenient to us at a certain time, or if it is different than what we wish it to be; what is right or wrong will remain so, regardless of what we choose to do about it.

Imagine that you have an appointment for an interview tomorrow at an unfamiliar location. You need to get there by a certain time. In order to achieve this, you consult a map. Once you establish the distance to your destination, you can estimate how long it might take you to get there. By now you can establish at what time you must leave your house in order to get to your appointment on time. You have a roadmap for your way. This does not mean that you will in fact do what needs to be done. You may leave on time or not. That is a choice you make. But if you didn't have a map, and you didn't know how long the trip might take, how could you possibly even have the slightest chance of finding your way to your interview, let alone arrive there on time? Ethics provides the roadmap; the choice to follow it is yours.

So where do we find this map? How do we know where to look for this guiding philosophy? When dealing with moral principles and values we may feel as if we were moving in the realm of abstract thoughts and ideas. As Christians, we are fortunate that our guiding philosophy has a living example; not just in the teachings but in the life of Jesus Christ. It is in His teachings and actions that we learn the guiding principles that will define the roadmap for our lives. Our purpose is to live our lives as Jesus lived His. We will certainly not be perfect, and will not succeed every time. This doesn't mean that the rules can be changed or that the standards can be lowered. It does mean, however, that having this roadmap allows us to recognize when we take a wrong turn, it gives us the opportunity to stop and go back to resume our journey on the right road.

The basic guiding principles concerning Christian Ethics are found in the New Testament in the teachings of Jesus and the Apostle

Paul. How Christian Ethics should determine behavior is captured best in Paul's letter to the Christians at the Church in Colossae: "And whatever you do, do it all in the name of the Lord Jesus, giving thanks to God the father through him." (Colossians 3:17 NIV) I invite you to read this verse slowly and think about it for a moment. Whatever you do - all of it - absolutely everything. A good student of history may think of Saint Augustine's proposition: "Love God and do as you please". Conversely, the pagan may suggest that you can: "Do as you please in spite of God". To the believer, however, it is plain to see that the Apostle Paul has the correct idea. The scope of his command applies to all of life. To Paul, as to all of us, our Lord Jesus Christ lays claim to every aspect of our thoughts and actions. It is not conceivable to leave any aspect outside of this claim. Could we follow Christ only in our thoughts, though not in our actions? Could we be Christians on Sundays but not during the rest of the week? How could we possibly draw a line in our lives to separate the areas that belong to Christ from those that do not? As Christians we are whole and complete in the love of our Lord. As such, we give ourselves to Him, whole and complete.

Whereas Paul's guiding principle places emphasis on the individual, Jesus' life shows behavior that is all inclusive: the personal, the social and the world at large can be seen through His parables and the beatitudes. What is particularly exhilarating about finding our guidance in this way is that we can learn ethics in action. We can clearly see how the purpose for our life is meant to be fulfilled. We have a beacon of light in Jesus, to show us the way out of our clutter and confusion. Our behavior tells who we are. By allowing Christian Ethics to guide our behavior, we become exemplary Christians.

Have you ever assembled a puzzle? When we open the box we find hundreds of little cardboard cutouts that, if combined in the right way, will reveal the picture shown on the cover of the box. It is a game of patience and persistence. In the process of picking the next piece, the way to identify the right one is to know what shape we are looking for. We can tell if the piece will fit or not. By picking each piece according to the shape we know will fit, our puzzle takes the shape of the intended picture. By taking every step according to the shape that Christ gave to His life, we live our lives in His light. A candle doesn't have a flame because it illuminates, but it illuminates because it has a flame. In the same way we become a beacon to others who see the light of the Holy Spirit reflected in our lives. When we become followers of Jesus, all the pieces of the puzzle in our lives fall collectively into place.

By learning about the life of Jesus and reflecting on His example we create points of reference to which we can come back to in times of doubt. Let me give you an example of the way this applies to your practical, everyday choices. A man is taking a leisurely walk along a river on a placid afternoon. He hears a cry for help. He sees a man, obviously in trouble, being pulled downstream by the strong current. The onlooker's instinct tells him to remain in the safety of the shore. The man's instinct is a powerful force. It does not require any effort on his part. It comes to him automatically. Let's suppose that this man does not posses any ethical values. He goes on about his business and doesn't think twice about the drowning man. He suffers no conflict, because his conscience is not aware of any higher plain than that of his own instinct, a close equivalent to the laws of nature. Let's suppose now that this same man is a Christian. He has learned to follow Jesus and knows of the parable of the Good Samaritan (Luke 10; 25-37). Jesus told the story of the man who was robbed and left wounded by the side of the road. A priest and a Levite passed him without stopping. It was one Samaritan who stopped and tended to his recovery. In this seemingly simple exchange we learn a deep principle. Jesus asks us who of the three proved to be a neighbor to the man who fell into the robbers' hands. We know the answer in our hearts. There is one person in need, and another person is aware of this need. The only conceivable course of action is to help. Going back to our swimmer, the Christian man, having Jesus' teachings to follow, he without hesitation comes to the rescue of the drowning man. It is his guiding principles, his inner quest of doing what is right, that compels him to abandon his safety and risk injury, or possibly his life, in an attempt to rescue the man in distress. Now let me ask you a question: If it was you being pulled downstream by the powerful current, who would you rather have walk by? The first onlooker or the second man, the Christian?

Translate this same thought into the greater scope of our social environment. We interact with each other on the assumption that we share a set of values and principles. We hope that when we are in need, the person or group of people who has the power to help us will follow our same roadmap. Otherwise communication would be hopeless, we would be speaking a different language.

It is our responsibility to be a worthy participant in our community and in our inner circle of friends and family. It is our duty then, as individuals, to learn this guiding philosophy and be deeply familiar with it, so that we will know how to act when we are called to apply it. It is our duty as Christians to learn from Jesus and follow him, in all our imperfections, to apply his teaching in "whatever we do". Once we know His way, the choice is then ours to follow Him or not. Just like a roadmap, the guiding philosophy is there and it is our decision to walk in its light, or live in the shadows. Following this road requires courage. The choices are not simple and there are grave consequences at stake. We often don't want to look at what we need to do because it is too painful to see, and we choose avoidance as a way to numb the pain. The way of Jesus is neither soft nor indulgent. It does not care how dangerous or difficult it is for us to follow. But it is through these tough times that we define who we are. It is the decisions that we make in difficult conditions that chisel our characters and give form to our own picture in the puzzle. Each time we avoid the good road, we loose a piece of ourselves, but every time we choose to follow Jesus, we bring light into the world. "Whoever believes in me, as the Scripture has said, streams of living water will flow from within him" (John 7:38). By following Jesus we not only bring love into our hearts, but into the life of others who may be lost in the darkness, having no roadmap to follow. People often try to invent a set of values of their own. Be it wealth, prestige, power, appearances, they build a hall of mirrors that gives them a false sense of direction. But in these self-focused worlds there is always some fatal flaw. When the foundations shake and the mirrors shatter, the individual is left alone, without any means to make himself whole again. There is no such thing as peace or true happiness away from God. This is what Jesus came down to tell us, while he lived among us. Jesus showed us right from wrong, and what it is that makes right

"right", and makes wrong "wrong". He showed us how to build our lives on strong foundations, such that they cannot be shattered.

It is through His ultimate sacrifice for us, that we have access to eternal life. Because he laid down his life on our behalf, we have a chance to enter the Kingdom of Heaven, invoking His name. This is a concept that may be difficult to understand, if we try to rationalize it. What we *can* do, however, is to study the life of Jesus and his teachings.

Imagine you have never been to Paris, and I show you some videos of my visit there. Paris sounds like a nice place, so you get some guidebooks and some maps and you do some reading on your own. You read many different accounts of the same place, written by different people. Even though you have never *been* to Paris, you have no doubt that it exists, and you would recognize it if you ever saw it. In order to know Jesus we need to surrender our own self-imposed limitations and come to Him with an open mind, like a child. It may require taking down some of the "mirrors" that you have built in your life, in order to see the true road.

In short, Christian Ethics is the study and application of the eternal and unbending teachings of the New Testament as exemplified in the life of Jesus Christ, and applied to the daily living of the believer in every aspect of life without exception or interruption.

3. Jesus as Embodiment and Exemplar of the Ideal Value System

An Introduction to Christian Ethics

The renowned German phenomenologist Max Scheler (1874-1928) was well known for his penetrating insight into the thorny problems related to judging the moral rightness of human behavior and actions. Several of his major works were wholly dedicated to the task of creating ethical systems in which human behavioral tendencies could be evaluated. However, despite worldwide recognition as an expert on the subject of ethics, Scheler's own prodigious history of moral transgression was common knowledge among the members of the philosopher's circle of colleagues and associates.

When confronted with the irrefutable fact of his troubling proclivity towards hedonism and its apparent opposition to the staunch system of morals and ethics that he advanced in his scholarly work, Scheler is reported to have replied that "the sign that points to Boston doesn't have to go there." In Scheler's worldview, his ability to formulate and justify complex systems dictating how people should act in order to best maintain ethicality was in no way impeded by his own apparent unwillingness to adhere to such strict standards of behavior.

Although this anecdote may be apocryphal, it effectively serves to illustrate one of the most crucial points of divergence between the study of ethics in a broader philosophical sense and the distinct characteristics of a specifically Christian approach to ethics that follows the example set forth by Jesus Christ. In the realm of secular scholarship, ethicists often view behaviors and actions outside of a real-world context, speculating about potentialities and outcomes as if in an experimental test tube, as it were, completely separated from the consequences and influences of everyday life. In this type of speculative ethical inquiry, fueled by logical syllogisms and emotionally detached rationality, it is entirely conceivable that the developer of a framework of ethical "shoulds" might elect not to adhere to the approach he or she had formulated.

For Christians, however, this type of intellectual compartmentalization is not advisable, as evidenced by the myriad prohibitions against hypocrisy that can be found throughout the Scriptures (e.g. Isaiah 29:13, Luke 6:41-2, Matthew 23:13, Titus 1:16). Indeed, the true significance of Christian ethics is the necessary correspondence between the abstract system of principles set forth in scripture and doctrine and the decisions, choices, and actions that one undertakes in navigating daily life. The life of Jesus Christ stands as the ultimate example of a dynamic, nuanced, profoundly meaningful embodiment of Christian ethics, demonstrating the absolute inseparability of theory and practice in this unique ethical framework. Using Christ's life and teachings as an ideal exemplar, this discussion will seek to delineate and explain the most salient principles and practices that comprise Christian ethics.

While many ethical principles can be distilled from the example of Jesus' life and teachings as set forth throughout the New Testament, most of these principles can be viewed as stemming from the two core premises of the Christian ethical framework, often called the Great Commandments, which are set forth in Mark 12:28-34. These principles exhort believers to love God absolutely and to love one's neighbor as oneself. Despite variations, virtually all of the ethical guidelines set forth in Christian doctrine (particularly in the New Testament) can be traced back to these principles.

Ethics are commonly regarded as the fundamental principles against which a person judges his or her potential actions. The study of ethical principles without a corollary emphasis on actions would amount to little more than an intellectual exercise. Interestingly, though, Jesus' statements on ethical principles are more often directed towards the steps the individual must take in directing spiritual or emotional disposition and temperament than in dictating specific rules for behavior.

Indeed, throughout the New Testament, ethical codes that are overly concerned with proscribing specific actions are repeatedly scorned as being removed from genuine spirituality. This is most clear in His harsh recrimination of the excessive prescriptivism practiced by the Pharisees (cf. Matthew 23:23, 25-26). A key characteristic of Christian ethics, therefore, is that the believer is expected to engage in active reflection, introspection, and mental self-talk ensuring a proper attitude towards God and fellow people. If a principled ethical outlook based on the Great Commandments is achieved and actively maintained, Jesus' teachings suggest, ethical actions, behavior, and choices will necessarily result.

While this directive may seem simple, the record of Jesus' life as set forth in the New Testament demonstrates that embodying a uniquely Christian ethical mindset is a practice that is comprised of a great many component behaviors, actions, and attitudes, including humility, charity, mercy, and, most importantly, unconditional love. Although these traits and attributes would be commendable as displayed in any context, they attain a more profound level of meaning when they are framed within the larger ethical system that Jesus sets forth in His teachings. In this context, all of these values can be regarded as manifestations of the two Great Commandments to love God and to love one another absolutely and without reservation. Within the system of Christian ethics, the act of aspiring to emulate and embody the principles that Christ demonstrated and discussed transcends the level of mere good deeds and aspires toward the fulfillment of a higher, overarching purpose.

Another notable characteristic of the system of ethics set forth by Jesus is the fact that His Biblical statements do not frequently address the nature of sins, or morally proscribed acts. Instead, as alluded to previously, Jesus' words in the New Testament led us to believe that He was more concerned that believers focus on attaining a pure spiritual attitude and outlook than in avoiding certain, specific actions and behaviors.

Similarly to His position on cultivating ethicality, Jesus repeatedly suggests that the action of transgressive sins springs out of mental, emotional, and attitudinal failure than on specific behavioral lapses. As such, many of the statements that Jesus makes regarding sins or moral failures address the negative patterns of thought and opinion that tend to lead towards such behaviors. This theme in Jesus' teaching on sin is related to His oft-repeated conviction that one's thoughts and beliefs are extremely important in cultivating an ethical stance.

While Jesus clearly does not over-sentimentalize the inherent ethicality of humans, His teachings also reflect His abiding faith in the ability of humans to overcome their sinful tendencies through concerted mental, emotional, and spiritual focus. Further, the comparatively minimal amount of emphasis that Jesus' teachings give to the concept of sin reveals the essentially optimistic nature of His ethical framework for Christian believers. Jesus' chief purpose in laying out a system of ethics was creating a path for the redemption of humanity, rather than advancing an ethics that essentially amounts to a system of condemnation and punishment (cf. John 3:17).

Because love for one another and the infinite value of every person in the eyes of God are the twin pillars of Jesus' ethical system, another important manifestation of the Christian ethical system is equal and considerate treatment of all people, regardless of their abilities, social status, material wealth, or station in life. The Beatitudes famously codify this principle by asserting the value of all people in the eyes of God, especially those who belong to marginalized or downtrodden social groups. Therefore, another important aspect of a Christian approach to ethics involves a deep and abiding respect for all people without regard for their social or material status (or lack thereof). Further, the ethical principles that Jesus both explained and manifested in His own behavior were oriented towards the removal of artificial divisions that tend to undermine the unity, harmony, and mutual regard that is a key element of Christianity.

Earlier in the discussion, the observation was made that Jesus' teachings and deeds did not heavily emphasize sin, but rather, chose to emphasize the redemptive potential for those who sought to live according to the principles of Christian ethics. Related to this is the parallel fact that Jesus did not often make the explicit connection between acting in an ethical, principled manner in the earthly realm and the potential for eternal salvation. While many of Jesus' statements do discuss eternal existence transcending death in the afterlife, He rarely expressed a direct, causative link between ethical behavior on earth and the promise of eternal life.

One of the more cynical deconstructions of Christian ethics that has been introduced over the years is the inference that Christian morality is, in actuality, little more than the behavior that is extracted from believers under duress as an inducement to attain entrance into heaven. In other words, it has often been asserted, most often by the most vocal of non-believers, that Christian ethics are often not a genuine expression of fundamental compassion and loving kindness, but instead are simply a false front concealing the self-serving desire to transcend physical death.

While it is inevitable that over the last two millennia there have been Christians whose ethical behavior is motivated largely or solely by the promise of an afterlife, this is not the inducement that emerges from a close reading of Jesus' own teachings. Throughout the New Testament, Jesus consistently emphasizes the personal and spiritual well being that can be attained through an assiduous dedication to cultivating ethical principles.

Indeed, upon a detailed examination of the Gospels, it becomes clear that there are far more references in Jesus' remarks to fostering spiritual fulfillment and community good will through an adherence to ethical values than there are references that directly link ethical behavior and eternal life. This observation supports a common interpretation that has been advanced by theologians in recent years, namely, that part of the "Kingdom of Heaven" that Jesus often refers to was the sense of well-being, virtuousness, and fulfillment that can be attained within each individual believer through a life-long dedication to promoting and adhering to a Christian system of ethics.

While the promise of life after death is a major component of the covenant between God and believers, many scholars point out that the references Jesus often made to the "Kingdom of Heaven" have as much to do with the personal spiritual fulfillment of living ethically as with the conveyance to a separate realm in the afterlife. This belief can be traced to pre-Christian doctrine in the Jewish tradition, which emphasized good works and ethicality without focusing extensively upon the specific promise of an eternal reward for earthly behavior.

Although the connection between ethical actions on Earth and eternal life is an important doctrinal issue, there are many more pressing concerns that Christians must address in applying Christian ethics. Perhaps the most profound challenge that believers face in seeking to live and act within a framework of Christian ethics is reconciling the teachings and actions of Jesus with the harsh realities of our own contemporary cultural and social context. Because the secular norm of socially expected behavior has come to diverge so sharply from the ethical standards set forth by Jesus, finding a path that balances a faith-based ethicality with deference and loyalty to society and the community can often prove to be an extremely arduous task.

However, in spite of the fact that Jesus' teachings of unconditional love, mercy, and compassion were highly radical in His own historical context, many of His statements directly address the problem of cultivating ethical behavior in a secular society that values outward status and material wealth above all else (cf. Matthew 19:24, Luke 12:16-21, Mark 10:25). Jesus, too, was forced to reconcile the tenets of His faith within a particular social, cultural, and historical moment.

Ultimately, Jesus' message of Christian ethics proved to be too threatening to the status quo, and He paid for His nonconformity with His human life. However, for the most part, Jesus' teachings throughout the New Testament seek to forge equilibrium between adherence to Christian ethical principles and the exigencies of the quotidian world in which we live. Christian ethics can undoubtedly be applied in an imperfect world. Indeed, the deeper meaning of the Christian approach to ethics is the determination of believers to blend abstract ethical principles within the context of an often-unwelcoming secular society. We can achieve this by following the example of Jesus, who wholly embodied the ethical doctrine He espoused in His behaviors and actions.

4. Ethics in the Early Church

Another Important Framework of Ethical Behavior for Christians

One of the most significant challenges for current-day Christians is the process of developing a moral system that is based on Christian principles, but can also be applied in many real-life situations. Clearly, the exemplar of Jesus Christ must necessarily serve as the most important ethical model for believers. Within His actions and teachings as set forth within the New Testament, the most important fundamental principles of Christian ethics are exemplified. Believers seeking to live their own lives according to Christian ethical principles should rightly aspire to emulating the ethicality embodied perfectly in Jesus Christ.

Realistically, however, it can be difficult, sometimes well nigh impossible, to consistently manifest the Christ-like ethical behavior demonstrated by the Lord in the New Testament. While Jesus is, by definition, the ultimate ethical exemplar for all Christians, the fact remains that He was blessed with a spirituality that far exceeds our own moral and ethical resources. Indeed, the formidable prospect of exemplifying Christ-like ethicality has been so daunting to some believers that rather than facing the challenge, they turn away from Christianity altogether. While this recourse is highly misguided, it serves to demonstrate the difficulty that many perceive in living one's life in perfect accord with the example set forth by the Son of God.

Although Jesus and His ethical principles are of primary importance to Christians, it must be acknowledged that His life was something of a special case. In other words, even as accounts of His ethical beliefs and principles are highly important to Christians, there is often a perceived distance between the exemplar of Jesus and our own actions in daily life because of the conditions and context specific to His existence and the special challenges that He faced as the incarnate Son of God.

For this and other reasons, it can be instructive to look to the biblical accounts of the Early Church as a means of supplementing the ethical exemplar of Jesus. Although Jesus was human and, as a result, felt many of the doubts and hesitation that humans often experience in the process of living a life based on Christian principles, the actions and behaviors of the early Church members are even more recognizable to us as eminently human. The fact that most of the early Church members were able to overcome their weaknesses and live a spiritual life so closely attuned to the example of Jesus can be very inspiring to current-day Christians seeking to revitalize their personal ethical compasses.

This discussion will present an overview of the ethical principles set forth and embodied by the early members of the Church. A particular focus will be upon demonstrating the ways that these early Christians sought to exemplify Christ's ethical teachings in their lives and communities. In conclusion, an assessment of the significance of the ethical example of the early Church for current-day Christians will be presented.

Although there are many models of ethical principles and behavior that are set forth in the biblical accounts of the early Church, perhaps the most widely accepted accounts are those set forth by Paul. His account of the early Church and the ethical principles by which the nascent Christian community sought to live presents a compelling example for current-day believers seeking to apply Christian ethical beliefs in a real-world environment. Admittedly, the historical, social, and cultural context in which the early Church existed differ quite significantly from the contemporary context. However, Paul's examples still present an important alternative model for the application of Christian ethical principles by a church community that existed in very close historical proximity to Jesus Christ.

The main emphasis that Paul relates in discussing the role of ethics in the early Church is the primary importance of the fulfillment of Jesus' commandment to love one's neighbor as oneself. For Paul, this stricture defines the most significant aspect of Christian ethicality, and his account of the early Church consequently foregrounds the community's efforts to achieve an environment in which mutual loving kindness, respect, and esteem are the defining characteristics.

Paul's principles also emphasize the importance of cultivating Christ-like ethicality in daily life. To him, the striving towards this admittedly impossible goal is the single behavior that defines

Christian ethics. Although some detractors interpret Paul's teachings as highly narrow and prescriptive, his own interpretation is that the emphasis in Christian ethics should be upon the ideal principles, rather than endless lists of rules and prohibited behaviors.

This sentiment on Paul's part is similar to Jesus' own complaints against the legalistic mindset of the Pharisees. For both Jesus and Paul, adhering to the fundamental principles of love, mutual respect, and reciprocal regard are more important than living by predefined rules of ethical behavior. Indeed, Paul further expounds upon this by asserting that the most important duty of Christians consisted of applying these fundamental ethical principles to an ever-shifting array of real-world scenarios and dilemmas. Within such a demonstration of interpretive sagacity, Paul asserts, lies the true mark of an ethical Christian.

Whereas the teachings of Paul tend to emphasize the importance of applying Christian principles in real-life situations, the teachings of another important figure in the early Church, John, have a more mystical bent, delving into the philosophical aspects of the ethical principles exemplified through Jesus. In the account set forth by John, the achievement of a fully realized Christian ethicality is attained through a process of spiritual transformation. In a moment of epiphany, believers will be granted access to the spiritual enlightenment that will allow them a heightened ability to understand and apply ethical principles in their daily life.

Whereas Paul emphasized the repeated choices to act in an ethical manner in a variety of real world situations as the most important aspect of following Christ's ethical example, John figures this process as a much more ephemeral component of a larger spiritual transformation that cannot be attained solely through consistent behavior. For John, Christian ethics is a part of the mystical element of faith, and it cannot simply be achieved through adhering to certain principles. Instead, this process is part of a larger, essentially mysterious spiritual transformation. Still, John does acknowledge the necessity of applying ethics in a real-world framework, as indicated by his recognition of the difficulties of acting ethically in the face of the extreme persecution that early Church members were often forced to withstand from non-believers.

Perhaps the single most important crystallization of the ethical behavior of the early Christians is seen in the book typically attributed to Luke, the Acts of the Apostles. Throughout this book, the author presents a historical account of the actions, behaviors, beliefs, and principles of the earliest Church members. One passage that famously encapsulates the ethical values of the early church community is Acts 2:42-47, in which the core ethical principles of the early Church are specifically addressed.

In this passage, it is stated that the early Church members "had all things common [...] and sold their possessions and goods, and parted them to all men, as every man had need." From this, it can be extrapolated that the early Church members radically exemplified the ethical principles that Christ had set forth, so much so that they went against common social principles of individual property and self-service. This example is particularly important because it underscores the need for Christians, even today, to critically assess prevailing social norms and their compatibility with the ethical teachings of Jesus.

As demonstrated by this passage in Acts, the early Church members adopted an approach to manifesting Christian ethics that was so divergent from prevailing social norms that they were often ostracized and persecuted for it. At the same time, their ability to embody Christ's teachings and live in accord with Christian ethical principles served as an extremely successful exemplar for converts to Christianity, as indicated by the rapid growth of the Church and its membership during this period.

While biblical sources are often regarded as the most doctrinally significant examples of the ethics of the early Church, extracanonical texts can also be used to supplement the rather minimalist account of early Church life that is provided in the Bible itself. Although it goes without saying that these supplemental texts should not be treated with the same reverence afforded for canonical books of the Bible, these historical accounts from early Church members and contemporary observers also help to demonstrate the ways in which the ethical teachings of Jesus Christ were exemplified by the early Christians.

These extracanonical accounts further substantiate the portrait of the early Church as a close-knit community that was drawn together through a shared reliance on the ethical principles of Jesus. Virtually every account given of the early Church refers to the extraordinary bonds between the community members. Even in the face of rapid growth, the group truly seemed to function as a unified whole that happened to be comprised of individual members similarly dedicated to the dissemination of the Gospel.

In order to successfully overcome the extremely formidable challenges they faced in hostile Jewish and pagan communities, the early Church members banded together in shared respect of Jesus' ethical teachings. Even the skeptical accounts that are antagonistic towards the early Christians grudgingly make note of the extent to which the Church members exemplified in their daily lives the doctrinal teachings and ethical principles that they advanced in Christ's name. All who encountered the early Church members were impacted by the degree of conformity between their ethical principles and their daily actions in life.

Another common element of the extracanonical writings on the ethics of the early Church is the move away from the more abstract, principle-based ideology that is set forth in Scripture and a turn towards the legalistic prescriptivism that Christ and most of the early Church fathers explicitly decried. The non-canonical writers that chronicled the early Church often tended to try to distill the core ethical values of Christianity into lists of "do's and don'ts," reducing the core principles of mutual regard and loving kindness into more facile, but easily understandable rule books.

While both Jesus and Paul emphasize the importance of individual judgment in applying Christian ethical principles to real life situations, the centuries following the establishment of the Church saw an increase in the number of rule-based interpretations of Christian ethics and proper behavior. As the flocks of Church members increased precipitously during this period, it became more difficult to maintain the sense of shared community that so defined the earliest group of Christians. As a result, many Church groups moved away from the principle of applying core ethical values in different ways as the situation demanded, and towards rules-based systems that did not allow for such discretion on the part of the individual believer. To some extent, these rules-based systems continue to be prevalent today, particularly in more fundamentalist sects. Many current-day Christian communities adhere to lists of dictated "do's and don'ts" rather than encouraging members to apply the core dictums of Christ's simple ethical principles – mutual regard, loving kindness, and reciprocal respect – to daily situations as they emerge. In this way, much of the discretionary aspect Christian ethics that was common in the early Church has been virtually eradicated from current practice.

However, if one takes the example of ethics in the early Church that is presented through scriptural and extracanonical accounts, it is clear that the emphasis should be placed upon creating a close-knit, interdependent church community that is primarily concerned with exemplifying Christian ethics, both in principle and in practice. Rather than closely following lists of dictates prescribed by pastoral leaders, those seeking to follow the ethical example of the early Church members will place their faith in their own ability to embody Christ's simple but profound ethical values. Jesus trusted the early Church members to make ethical decisions based on their personal interpretation of His ethical teachings. Perhaps the strong sense of community and solidarity that was a defining characteristic of the early Church could be restored if more current-day Christians sought to emulate this example.

5. What Would Jesus Do?

Advantages and Problems of Situational Ethics for Christians

Based on the teachings of Jesus, in addition to the accounts of the early Church that are provided by Paul, Luke, and other canonical and non-canonical writers, we see that the early approach to Christian ethics was largely based upon adherence to a few simple principles that Jesus reiterated repeatedly in His teachings. Jesus asked that His followers love one another and treat each other with the same respect and regard that they hoped for themselves. A close reading of the New Testament reveals that the wide array of parables and examples that Jesus provides in His ethical teachings can all be viewed as variations on these important themes.

Paul, too, saw the importance in advancing a few essential ethical principles as the core of the Christian's daily practice. However, His writings begin to show the tendency towards substituting specific laws and rules for a more independent reliance on one's personal ability to make good ethical choices in the course of daily life. While Paul repeatedly reiterates the essential vitality of Jesus' Great Commandments, the principles at the heart of New Testament Christian ethics, He also enumerates many specific practices that should be followed, or alternatively, avoided, in order to adhere closely to Christian doctrine.

Jesus, on the other hand, appeared to disdain more legalistic forms of ethical practice, as indicated by His invective against the Pharisees. Although the many parables that Christ used as teaching tools contained specific examples of actions to be cultivated and avoided, most current-day theologians view these more as symbolic embodiments of Christ's Great Commandments, rather than specific rules for Christian behavior.

Based on Christ's teachings in the New Testament, He repeatedly asserts that believers who adhere to the simple ethical framework He sets forth will be able to navigate daily life in a spiritually consistent manner. He asserts that the diligent Christian believer will be able to apply these ethical principles in a wide variety of common situations and make their own determination as to the most ethical course of actions. Therefore, the code of Christian ethics that Jesus sets forth is an unusual amalgamation of situational ethics – defined as an ethical system that relies on the context of a particular situation in order to make the best ethical decision – and absolutism – in which the same principles are applied in every situation.

However, there are significant points of contradiction that separate absolutism and situationism as ethical frameworks. Generally, absolutism is regarded as the only ethical system that is consistent with the application of a uniform set of ethical principles such as those which define Christianity. Further, situational ethics are often associated with ethical systems that are relative, i.e., do not subscribe to any consistent set of principles. Ethical relativism is, in the eyes of many current-day theologians, the antithetical opposite of Christian ethics.

How, then, do we account for the irrefutably situationist aspects of the ethical approach suggested by Christ himself in the New Testament? Further, what are we to make of the recent rise in the popularity of the ubiquitous situationist catchphrase, "What Would Jesus Do?" that has recently become a pervasive touchstone among younger Christians? Some in the community have celebrated the WWJD movement for its ability to make the presence of Christ a more immediate constant in the lives of young people attempting to make their way in an increasingly complex world.

Many conservative theologians, however, are bothered by the situationist implications of the WWJD movement, in that they see it as implying a level of situational relativism that may tend to tarnish the ethical consistency of the ideology set forth in Christ's New Testament teachings. Detractors equate wearing a "WWJD" T-shirt or bracelet with the implication that the wearer could possibly understand and predict the decision that the Son of God would make in any given situation.

This lesson will delve into the complex debate over applying situational and absolutist ethical frameworks to Christian ethical principles. Both the advantages and pitfalls of absolutist and situationist stances will be enumerated and discussed. In conclusion, the role of situational ethics within the larger context of absolutist Christian ethics will be assessed.

Throughout the twentieth century, the debate between situationism and absolutism has been one of the most defining controversies among opposing camps of Christian theologians. Confounding the controversy is the fact that the New Testament can be interpreted as supporting both approaches to ethical behavior.

Because the system that Jesus endorses throughout His New Testament teachings contains elements of both situationism and absolutism, there has been no definitive conclusion as to the correct approach for Christian believers to take in making ethical choices. Generally, the debate has devolved into a partisan contest between conservative and liberal sects of the Church, with conservative groups promoting the use of absolutist Christian ethics, and liberal factions promoting a situational Christian ethics.

The side in the debate that holds that Christian ethics are, by definition, a type of absolutism points out that there is an underlying set of principles that are held to be objectively and eternally true. Proponents of Christian absolutism argue that, for example, there could never be a conceivable situation in which the Great Commandment to love one's neighbor as oneself would no longer apply.

Christ repeatedly asserted that a primary condition for faithful Christian living was a consistent adherence to the principles He set forth. As such, it stands to reason that Christian ethics could be construed as a form of absolutism, because the same core group of ethical principles must always be applied in the course of making ethical decisions in the course of daily life. Because Jesus insisted that loyal observance of these core principles formed the cornerstone of faithful Christian life, it must be acknowledged that there is little room for relativism when it comes to applying the ethical principles that Jesus enumerated as the most important values that distinguish believers from non-believers.

From this perspective, it seems clear that Christianity is an ethical framework that is based on absolute ideological principles. However, a similarly strong and persuasive argument can also be made for ethical situationism as the core ethical model advanced by Jesus throughout the New Testament.

As stated, many liberal interpretations of Christian ethics argue that Jesus' core ethical principles can be distilled down to a few basic principles that are applied differently in a plethora of varying situational contexts. The most prevalent situationist interpretation of Christian ethics that has gained widespread currency in recent years is the notion that Jesus' intent was only that His followers apply loving kindness, selflessness, and mutual respect and regard in every situation that arises.

Indeed, the sheer variety of potential ethical dilemmas, paired with the judgment ability of the individual believer, problematizes the assumption that Christian ethical values will be able to be applied with absolute equanimity in every situation. This, paired with Jesus' own frequent exhortations to followers to rely on their own faith as a beacon in ethically challenging situations, gives some weight to the claims of those who support situationist applications of Christian ethical principles.

In principle, the assertion that Christians must only apply love in every situation in order to behave ethically is very appealing. Many of Jesus' own statements can be interpreted as supporting this position, and it brings an elegant simplicity to the formidable responsibilities that Christian faith often bestows upon its adherents. It is comforting to think that love is all that is necessary in order to act in an ethical manner that is consistent with the requirements of Christian doctrine.

However, even the most cursory critical examination of this argument reveals its many weaknesses and deficiency. First, anyone who has attempted to make their way through the world using Christian principles will immediately recognize that many situations require a more complex, nuanced response than "love."

Second, despite the universal similarities that yoke together the nearly infinite spectrum of interpretations of Christian doctrine, it is nearly impossible for even two like-minded believers to agree on a definition of ethically correct Christian love. Postlapsarian human beings are necessarily flawed, and from the point of view of Christian ethics, part of our flawed nature is our individual subjectivity that disallows us from reaching universal understanding of God's approach to ethicality. One person's interpretation of a response that demonstrates ethical Christian love may be vastly different from those of another believer, and as such, relying on situational ethics to guide our behavior seems to be a rather risky proposition, due to the large amount of discretion and latitude it grants to each individual.

Perhaps the most troubling aspect of the increasingly popular situational Christian ethics is the fact that such a system minimizes the role of God as the infallible moral authority and places a large amount of authority in the individual believer. When one argues that individuals should be granted the ability to determine how best to apply Christian love in any given ethical dilemma, the implication is that humans can wield the moral authority of God.

Although Jesus' teachings consistently emphasize the role of individual discretion and personal responsibility in making ethical decisions, His first demand is absolute loyalty and faith in God. Therefore, it is misguided for proponents of situationist Christian ethics to wrest this moral authority from God and place it in the hands of the individual believer. This approach tends to undermine the single most important stricture of Christianity, namely, unconditional recognition and obedience to God's sovereignty.

Taken together, it would seem that there is biblical and doctrinal support for both the situationist and absolutist position in applying Christian ethics. Both sides in the debate have amassed substantial collections of scriptural support in order to demonstrate the correctness of their own position. However, when critically reviewed, the New Testament scriptural evidence is ambiguous, simultaneously supporting both approaches to ethical Christian decision-making. Ironically, some of the same biblical incidents recounted in the New Testament are often applied as support for both positions in the debate.

One of the most frequent examples that is cited in the debate over situationism versus absolutism is the incident recounted in Matthew 12, in which an important law of the era has been flouted when the disciples eat wheat from a field on the Sabbath. When the Pharisees decry this act as sacrilegious, Christ jumps to the defense of the disciples by bringing up the example of David, who in a crisis ate the special bread that was intended only for those in the priesthood.

Situationists have seized upon this example to demonstrate that Christ supported a position of at least partial relativism: as they interpret the incident in Matthew 12, Christ is asserting that even the most revered rules can be disregarded in special circumstances. From this argument, it has been further interpreted that Christ supported a stance of context-specific ethical decision-making. Some of the most ardent supporters of situationist Christian ethics have applied their conclusions from this incident to the entirety of the New Testament, devising a system in which contextual circumstances are as important a consideration as longstanding moral and religious laws.

At the same time, those in the absolutist camp have asserted that this incident should be dismissed as an example of Christ's masterful rhetoric. Elsewhere in the New Testament, Christ's disdain for the legalistic ethical system of the Pharisees has been amply established. As such, His defense of the disciples using an appeal to the nominalism of the Pharisees demonstrates only that He was crafting the most effective defense of the disciples available, rather than indicating Jesus' own belief in a system of situational Christian ethics.

Where do these seeming contradictions leave current-day believers seeking the best approach to applying Christian ethics in their walk through the world? Although believers typically approach Christian ethics on a situational, case-by-case basis, it is important that the ethical decision-making process be undertaken only in the context of affirming God's absolute moral authority. Appeals to situational relativism are inherently in contradiction with the Christian's duty to remain loyal to God in all things.

6. Ethics and Interpersonal Relations

Applying an Ethical Framework to Both Casual Interactions and Significant Relationships

The nature of developing and applying a Christian ethical framework dictates that one be able to apply complex, abstract principles that will be equally appropriate in a varied array of social interactions, ranging from a quick transaction in a convenience store to a lifelong relationship with a parent or a spouse. Because Christ exhorted His followers to love one's neighbor as oneself, each person that we encounter in our daily lives must be treated with the same level of regard and respect.

While it is important that Christians learn to apply a Christ-centered ethical framework in their interpersonal relationships, the most significant risk that we face is that of compartmentalizing and distinguishing between our "important" relationships and those more casual interactions that have no bearing on our life in the long-term. In order to truly foster a Christian ethical perspective, all of our interpersonal relations should ideally be informed by adherence to the New Covenant commandment to love one's neighbor as oneself.

This discussion will focus on the need to develop a workable, "portable" system of Christian ethics that can be applied in all of our interpersonal relations in order to bring glory to God and fulfill our responsibilities to love and respect our fellow human beings. Topics addressed will include the use of Scriptural principles as a means of developing a viable ethical framework for living, as well as referring to Christ's examples and teachings as an example for behaving ethically in our interpersonal relationships and casual daily interactions. In conclusion, an assessment of the need to act according to Christian ethical principles in all of our interpersonal relations will be made.

Because the scope of Christianity is so far-reaching and all-inclusive, there are many different Christian lifestyles that all serve, in their own unique ways, to manifest and illuminate the key tenets of the faith. However, there are certain universal elements that will always serve as a means of identifying and distinguishing a specifically Christian ethics and the corresponding lifestyle that is associated with this overarching perspective.

First and foremost, the most obvious point of divergence between Christians and their secular counterparts is the willingness of believers to flout social norms (and, if necessary, civil laws) in order to obey the Word of God. As such, Christians in our increasingly secular society are often subject to taunts and insults. Ironically, the more earnest, ethical, and principled a particular Christian individual is in his or her decision making and comportment, the more like he or she is to suffer ostracism and scorn from those in mainstream society. However, as was made clear by Jesus' teachings and examples, this scorn is no reason to seek to act differently, to camouflage one's belief system in the hopes of blending in with the proverbial crowd.

Jesus specifically warns His followers away from the ethical slippery slope of trying to act in an unethical but socially acceptable manner. In the example of Jesus' own life and death, His insurmountable drive to spread the Gospel resulted in His crucifixion at the hands of His tormentors. Still, throughout the New Testament, Jesus makes it clear that living in accordance with Christian ethical principles will likely result in ouster from the mainstream, despite the discomfort and personal pain that such estrangement will likely engender.

In some Christians, who, at some level, are not wholly committed to the process of adhering to a Christian ethical system regardless of the personal cost of such a step, this ostracism can result in a sense of inadequacy, existential loneliness, and self-pity. In order to successfully weather the social exclusion that is sometimes a byproduct of committing to an ethical Christian stance, believers must understand from the outset the point that Christ asserts repeatedly throughout the New Testament, namely, that to be Christian is to remove oneself from the worldly concerns of fitting in with mainstream society. In addition, if one is fortunate enough to be able to regularly participate in a supportive congregation, the fellowship of like-minded Christians can offer a profoundly meaningful comfort.

As a result of the relatively common social ostracism that Christians attempting to adhere to an ethical lifestyle often experience, there is often a tendency to cocoon into the congregation of sympathetic fellow believers and minimize contact with the "outside world." While the impulse behind such a move is certainly understandable, Christ did not intend the church community to be an insulated respite from the larger culture that one comes to wholly rely upon for social interaction (Philippians 3:20).

Indeed, resorting to this type of avoidance of the mainstream culture is actually counter to many of the statements that Christ makes regarding the need to promulgate the Gospel, both through direct evangelical activity, as well as simply by the virtue of one's hopefully positive and beneficial presence in the community. As Christians, we have an ethical obligation to walk in the world while simultaneously rejecting the claims of the world upon our spirit, heart, and mental perspective.

There are many other examples of characteristics of human relationships that are impacted according to the application of a system of Christian ethics. Although Christ acknowledged the necessity of facing the risk of social ostracism, He also repeatedly stresses the importance of cultivating healthy communication with one's family and loved ones, acting quickly to repair any problems, miscommunications, or arguments that may arise.

Indeed, one of the primary obstacles that can threaten one's ability to apply a Christian ethic in every aspect of life is simmering, unresolved anger. With this type of longstanding preoccupation sapping one's mental energy and concentration, it is often nearly impossible to muster the discipline and energy that is necessary to act in a manner consistent with Christian ethics and to withstand the social ostracism that can often arise from openly proclaiming one's belief system. Repeatedly, Christ warns against the myriad spiritual and emotional consequences of nursing longstanding resentment; instead, He urges His followers to reach out to estranged love ones and forge new connections with those from whom they have been separated.

One of the most important aspects of maintaining a healthy, developing relationship with God is being able to sustain the focus and spiritual attention necessary for such an intense and demanding undertaking. Those who are distracted by petty, unresolved quarrels with friends or family are typically ill equipped to create a deep and meaningful relationship with God.

Without sufficient spiritual focus upon the evolving relationship with God, one's ability to withstand the pressure of being, but not of, secular culture, is particular vulnerable to destruction. As such, the Christian's failure to cultivate positive, open, engaged interpersonal relations with friends and family can initiate a deleterious cycle of lack of spiritual focus, which in turn results in a lack of a meaningful relationship with God.

This is not to suggest that the process of cultivating a meaningful relationship with those around us is an effortless process. To the contrary, maintaining healthy human relationships can be an extremely daunting process, particularly for Christians who are forced to make the effort to reach out across the gap of skepticism and mistrust that may be harbored by non-Christian friends or family members.

However, the consistent application of a system of Christian ethics can be a helpful tool in minimizing the difficulties associated with navigating this treacherous terrain. By applying a consistent code of ethics to interpersonal relations, it is much easier to maintain adherence to doctrinal principles and to act in a way that is consistent with the tenets of the Christian faith. Because any action, behavior, or decision that is in violation or opposition of the express teachings of the Bible can be considered unethical from a Christian perspective, using these principles as a guiding standard can eliminate much of the ambiguity and confusion from sometimes-confounding human relationships.

One important ethical consideration for Christians in conducting their interpersonal relationships is maintaining a constant vigilance against tarnishing the sanctity of the body. While this might seem like a somewhat trivial concern in comparison with more substantial issues of ethics, Christ repeatedly reiterates the need to maintain one's body as a sacred temple. As a result, in making ethical decisions addressing interpersonal relationships, it is important to consider whether a potential course of action may tend to degrade one's body physically or, by extension, mentally. This issue should be of particular concern for Christians negotiating the always-precarious terrain of romantic and sexual relationships.

Because the concept of the body, rendered sacred by the presence of the Holy Ghost, extends to include the mental and spiritual components in the version set forth by Jesus in the New Testament, the Christian's ethical imperative to maintain the sanctity of the body extends far beyond sustaining the integrity of the physical body. Instead, it also should be regarded as including the mind, spirit, mental capacity, and emotional well-being.

Therefore, in applying principles of Christian ethics to interpersonal relations, Christians must remain cognizant of any relationship or association that may potentially threaten any of these aspects. The wife, for example, who elects to remain in the realm of a verbally abusive husband, is taking the risk of degrading her own mental and spiritual well-being, and thereby, violating Jesus' dictate to maintain the sanctity of the temple of the body. The ethically correct course of action would be to remain away from the relationship until the partner had received pastoral help in curbing his emotionally destructive behaviors.

On a related note, Jesus' exhortation to keep the temple of the body pure also conveys upon Christians the ethical responsibility of maintaining moderation in all their activities. As stated at several points in the Old Testament and the New Testament, the middle course of moderation is the most beneficial approach to adopt in maintaining the sanctity of the body.

This applies not only to the obvious categories of potential appetite, such as overeating, but also to any of a number of activities that may inspire immoderate behavior. Indeed, virtually any activity can be undertaken too often, resulting in an unhealthy preoccupation and sense of unbalance that can serve to threaten the sanctity of the body as dictated by Christ.

Therefore, another important ethical consideration that Christians must consider in guiding the course of their interpersonal relations is maintaining a conservative level of moderation in all things. This principle, consistently applied, will safeguard the body, the mind, and the spirit, all of which are vital components of the active, engaged Christian lifestyle (I Corinthians 10:31).

Another important ethical consideration that should play a role in the decision-making process for Christians is Jesus' insistence that Christians, while remaining loyal to the strictures of the faith, must also obey civil laws, insofar as they do not contradict the Word of

God. Jesus points out that the order that is achieved through adherence to civil laws is beneficial to society as a whole.

Our personal relationships, as well, should be cultivated and conducted with the larger good in mind. The network of relationships that typically surround each individual serves as an important microcosm of the larger society, and according to the Bible, tending to each of these interpersonal relations with care, sensitivity, loving kindness, and mutual respect and regard will benefit the society as a whole.

All of these ethical responsibilities can be encapsulated in the demand that Jesus repeats throughout the New Testament, namely, to do all things for the glory of God. While there are many other factors and variables that must play a role in the decision-making process of the Christian's ethical system, the final test for any potential course of action is the extent to which it will tend to bring glory to God. Each moment of our interactions with other individuals, ranging from inconsequential exchanges of small talk to our lifelong relationships with our spouses, should be designed to meet this all-important ethical criterion.

7. Ethics and Modern Politics

"The only thing necessary for evil to triumph
is for good men to do nothing."
E. Burke

In his Science of Right, Kant proposes that unless the very institution of right is to be renounced (as in giving up the right to own property, or the right to free speech), the first thing incumbent upon men is to accept the principle that it is necessary to leave the state of nature, in which each one follows his own inclinations, and to form a union of those who come into reciprocal communication, and to subject themselves in common to the external restraint of public law. In this way man enters into a civil union, and the act by which it constitutes itself into a state is termed the *original contract*. Before such a contract establishes a legal society, individual men can never be safe from violence to each other. By this civil contract the powers are conferred upon the sovereign which, according to the laws of freedom, can be no other than the people itself united into a nation. The dignities of the sovereign are given to the ruling power, whose function is to govern, by the constituents of the state, whose function is to obey. The people give up their external freedom in order to receive it immediately again as members of a nation.

I cannot think of a higher order for an individual, in civil life, than to be entrusted with the preservation of the rights and the freedom of the people of his nation. Such is the mandate of the politician. In a republic, constituted by the representative system, it is in the people that the supreme power resides. It is by the original contract, embodied by the ballot box, that this power is bestowed on elected officials. In the practice of politics, the individual enters the realm of general principles, which are no longer particular to him alone, but common to every citizen. These universal principles span across ideological and partisan platforms, and remain unchanged over time. The teacher, the worker, the housewife, the professional, each and every one entrusts their elected officials with the custodianship of these precious principles. There is an essential element of trust on the premise that the representative will fulfill the original contract, and a tacit understanding that the guardian of such a precious commodity will be held to the highest standards in order to merit such privilege. It is therefore not unreasonable to expect that politicians should hold a sincere commitment to these principles.

It occurs to me that in modern politics, the terms of the original contract have been set aside, and instead of the aim being the well-being of the people in a life of safety and freedom, what we are left with is a Machiavellian struggle for the allocation of privilege. Most of the founders of our nation portrayed a passion for their ideals and felt a stain in their characters as deeply as they would feel a physical wound. These days, unethical practices have become commonplace to the point that we, as a nation, are at risk of losing our sense of moral indignation and come to accept these aberrations as the norm. Politics has become a field where strategy and tactics of the "game of influence" have taken the place of ethics. The passionate leaders of earlier times have been replaced by individuals skilled in the art of compromise and accommodation to special interests.

This brings to mind the recent events surrounding the potential impeachment of the President. The rather distasteful case involved the President's lie under oath regarding his sexual involvement with a young lady who was working as an intern in the White House at the time. The media bombarded our collective attention with the particulars of this case every single day over a period of several months (which to some of us felt like years). At the climax of this very public saga, the President decided to speak directly to the nation in a televised address. Looking straight at the camera, speaking to the people that had elected him to fulfill the highest civil duty, from his seat in the White House, he roundly denied the allegations. As became evident in later events, the President was lying. The impeachment proceedings gradually tapered off and died, but the stain on his character was to remain. A public debate ensued and opinions flared; one argument in favor of "looking the other way" and focusing on the achievements of the administration, the other affirming that no one is above the law, not even the President. In my observation, the defining moment of this controversy, the single instance that drew a collective gasp, did not come with the lie under oath, in the formal proceedings of the prosecution, but in the moment when the President lied to his people with a straight face, a moment that directly penetrated the homes and hearts of millions through their televisions. There was a palpable disenchantment in the street, a sense that a certain ethical ground had been irretrievably lost. It was as if this singular public event had provided a snapshot into the moral order of the nation. Could it be that, as a society, this was a mirror reflecting to what extent our ethical values had decayed?

Aristotle states that moral virtue comes as a result of habit, and from this he concludes that none of the moral virtues arises in us by nature, but are learned and become perfect by their practice. Such is what happens in states, for legislators seek to make the citizens good by forming moral habits in them, and those who don't reach this challenge miss their mark, for it is in this dynamic that a good community differs from a bad one. He further proposes that we learn these habits by doing, just as a builder learns by building and a musician learns by playing, so we become just by doing just acts, and temperate by doing temperate acts. Yet confronted with the same appetites some men become temperate and others become self-indulgent and irascible. It follows then that there is an individual choice in the matter. Being that the state is formed by cities and villages which in turn are formed by households, Aristotle asserts that before speaking of the state we must speak of the household: it is the most familiar community unit, and the place where ethics begin. It is furthermore, the environment where values are taught and transmitted from one generation to the next. Much of what plays out later in the fields of politics has been learned in the family unit. It is in the household, therefore, that the citizen has the opportunity to instill values and virtues. It is by the examples of practicing these principles that the child learns them. The discussion of these matters in the home when the child is old enough to understand them provides the fertile ground where virtues bloom. A child will carry these guiding teachings with him wherever the future takes him. And here arises an interesting point, whether the virtue of a good man and that of the politician are the same. Do the ethical principles learned in the household apply to the grander stage of politics? I believe they do, and not only that, but the politician, because he is entrusted with the freedoms, ethical leadership and rights of his constituents, needs to exercise these virtues to the letter. The duties of the politician are more demanding than those of the common man, and so is the need for him to exercise the utmost care in preserving the ethical code of values. Politicians are therefore held to the highest standards. As has been well said, he who has never learned to obey cannot be a good commander. The politician in charge of deliberating and taking action on matters of law and state can hardly be expected to apply in his public life any principles that he does not already carry within him at the time he is appointed to office. It is just a matter of time before any shortcoming in this area becomes painfully evident as in the case of the imprudent statement by the Senate Majority Leader, paying tribute to the leader of a past racial segregationist cause. What incensed public opinion was his claim that if this racist cause had prevailed, our nation wouldn't have all the problems it has today. It is an understatement to say that his words were insensitive to the racial struggles that continue to divide the nation. Racial equality was probably not a value that was instilled in him in his youth, nor did he take this principle to heart in later life. But since current events have rendered this principle to be desirable in the public eye, he had attempted to conceal the fact that racism was a part of who he was. His racist words came out spontaneously, and I believe he may have been surprised by the effect they had. It has also become apparent that issues of ethics have become a bone of political contention. Rather than rejecting the unethical action for its nature, the focus is placed on the ground to be gained by the momentary loss of influence of the public official whose actions are being questioned. The Senator's oratorical blunder caught the news like wildfire and created an opening for his detractors, within his own party, who had been waiting for several years for the opportunity to effect a change in leadership. It should be noted, however, that the Senator's words were consistent with public remarks he had made in the past, and that he offered a public apology and a promise to atone for his mistake. If this politically incorrect statement was enough to remove him now, why had his position on the matter been overlooked in the past? The picture painted by the media was in black and white. Although the Senator's state had a higher number of elected black officials than any other, nothing was said of the Senator's role in this achievement. Rather than a case of moral outrage at the ethical issues at stake, this was the case of a faux pas being manipulated to achieve a desired outcome. In such cases the driving force of greed and personal advancement is disguised in self-righteous discourse. Rather than an ethical search for the right decisions, matters take on the nature of a mean-spirited political tug of war.

As a result of these ugly squirmishes, people retreat from these issues, potentially turning their backs on their own freedom. A commitment to active citizenship is a critical element required for social progress. To stand still, without participation in civil life, equates to an act of surrender to the forces of corruption in politics. Left unchecked, political corruption will lead to the disruption of the civic order, resulting in the loss of the freedom gained in the original contract. One of the fundamental theological concepts found in the scriptures is that of the Covenant. As in the instance of God and Israel, and Abraham, it carries the meaning of a binding relationship, one that involves an obligatory aspect. It is a relationship based on mutual commitment, which includes promises and obligations, and which has the qualities of reliability and durability. There are secular covenants, as between two heads of state, or between the King and his people, and sacred covenants, between God and His people. The Bible is full of mentions of politics: kings and empires - armies and wars. There is no systematic guideline as to political matters, and yet it emphasizes freedom and liberation. We find freedom in John 8:36 "So if the Son sets you free, you will be free indeed", and in Romans 8:21 "that the creation itself will be liberated from its bondage to decay and brought into the glorious freedom of the children of God". Freedom is an ever-present element in both the Old and New Testaments. Freedom is both a desirable effect as well as an obligation for Christians, commanding us to stand with the oppressed and the powerless and join them in their cry for deliverance. Neutrality is not offered as an option. It is therefore in our Christian values to strive for freedom and liberation. There is no possibility to sustain a set of "public ethics" separate from our private Christian values. Rather, our Christian values are made true by publicly upholding them. The Christian value of freedom is the one that we, as a community, have collectively relinquished in our original contract, our covenant, in order to regain it fully back as a nation. The covenant comes with obligations, not only for the rulers, but for the citizens too. Our obligation as good citizens is to participate actively in civic life and to raise our children with these values, in order to hold our end of the bargain.

After all, it is in what we accept as good and what we reject as wrong that the moral order of our society is reflected. When we acquiesce and become reconciled to a lower standard, we cheat ourselves and future generations of the right to pursue excellence. We are human, and we are all fallible. We have weaknesses and we are all susceptible to sin. But that is not the way it has to be. It is so only if we resign ourselves to it. Our only hope as a nation is to be bold enough to strive for what "ought to be" as opposed to "what is". If happiness is to live in accordance with virtue, then living in accordance to the highest virtue will be the best thing for us. Even if the attainment of ethical excellence remains forever a pious wish, we must anyhow work incessantly towards it, and adopt it as the guiding principle for our actions, as well as the standard to which our representatives are to be held. This is God's way. Can we dare do less?

8. Ethics and Economics

"The quest for riches darkens the sense of right and wrong".
Antiphanes

There is no other system in my view that has proven to be more effective than capitalism in the production and distribution of wealth. With all its flaws, I cannot conceive of a free society without the right to property, free enterprise and individual risk-taking. We can argue that capitalism has yet been unable to end poverty. We can add that the distribution of wealth in capitalist countries still follows the pattern of a great deal of gain in the hands of a few. All this is true. None of the alternatives, however, have yielded any better results to my knowledge. Take communism for example. In the process of stripping off the wealthy, it makes everyone poor. Its ubiquitous government involvement spills over to restrict individual freedom, and its leaders' preoccupation with maintaining power gets in the way of the welfare of their people. There may be a time when a better economic model is found, but at this time capitalism is my choice. Having lived all my life in a capitalist country, my treatment of the ethical principles of the acquisition and distribution of wealth stem naturally from that perspective. I believe however, that these principles are applicable to all people living under different economic and political systems.

As creatures of God, we must depend on Him to provide for us and meet our needs for material and spiritual nourishment. Jesus speaks to us in Mark 11:24 "Therefore I tell you, whatever you ask in prayer, believe that you have received it and it will be yours." At face value, it may seem very simple then, to merely ask forwhatever our heart desires, and watch it materialize before our eyes. The most intriguing words in this message are "believe that you have received it". This means: have such strong faith that in your heart, whatever it is that you are praying for is already an accomplished fact. This kind of faith is rare and close to holy. It is difficult for me to picture the holder of such grace asking for a new car, or a luxury vacation. I rather imagine this believer praying for health, wisdom and peace.

But is it necessarily wrong to desire mere material possessions? Every person has the right to the pursuit of happiness. And that pursuit takes as many shapes as the number of pursuers. You would be hard pressed to find two people who conceive the exact same vision of what happiness is. If you had a chance to have anything you want, what would be your wish? Your idea of wealth is probably different from mine, and most different from somebody who has either much less or much more than you have. It is a trap to think that it is morally wrong to be rich and morally right to be poor. In Mathew 19:24 Jesus teaches us that "… it is easier for a camel to go through the eye of a needle than for a rich man to enter the kingdom of God." His message implies that it is more likely that the rich man has made the pursuit of wealth the center of his life, rather than living for his relationship with God. I believe this is the reason why it would be less likely for a rich man to get to heaven, rather than the mere objective fact of their being rich isolated from its spiritual implication. Poverty in itself is no guarantee for our soul's salvation, and neither is wealth. This would imply that ambition and the desire to be prosperous and to advance your station in life is morally wrong. But without ambition and the need for self-actualization, the great enterprises which carry a great cost or risk would never be undertaken. Think of an example of someone you know, who has worked hard for years, or has had a great idea, and as a result enjoys a comfortable economic situation. Their endeavor has created jobs for countless families. The community has been favored with a new school or a new park. We cannot honestly argue that this has been a life of immorality. So we therefore come to the revelation that it is not wealth in itself that makes or breaks the moral man, but the role that such wealth plays in his life, and what the wealth is applied towards. Let us imagine now that this same person had squandered his wealth in superfluous luxuries while his employees were suffering unhealthy working conditions and economic deprivation. There is a line that has been crossed, but where is this line to be drawn? How much is enough and where does enough start to be too much? Consider this: the line has been crossed when more for us means less for somebody else.

In a capitalist society, the individual is constantly bombarded by intrusive messages to acquire more, better, greater things. Every gain eventually turns into something the individual takes for granted as the next better, greater thing comes along. The individual consumer loses his sense of direction, in the rushing currents of material acquisition. Somewhere between the two extremes of poverty and opulence there lies an ample area of comfortable abundance. But the individual blindly seeking the next acquisition is not able to enjoy this comfort. He doesn't even know that he has already arrived. And therefore the disquieting race for the ideal material situation continues. The attainment of material goods and status takes center stage and forces every other aspect of life into the background. The original dream is all but forgotten. Imagine that you are crossing a stream and take advantage of a few stepping-stones that can get you to the other side without danger of falling in. You take the first step, and then the next, until you begin to concentrate so much on the stepping-stones themselves that you lose your sense of direction. At this point you don't remember that the stepping-stones were a means to get to the other side. In the preoccupation with the next foothold, you don't even realize that you are walking around in circles. Such it is with material gain. One achievement leads to the next. A greedier dream keeps replacing the original one, and one after another a new mirage takes the seeker crashing into the next empty quest.

For those who live in a country where opportunities for material advancement are plentiful, there lurks the constant danger of falling into an ethical void of understanding, mistaking the stepping-stones for the destination. Wealth and power as the aim of life corrupt the spirit. At the point where more for us results in less for others, there needs to be a communal call for a return to our core values. There is wastefulness and excessive consumption of non-renewable resources. There is malnutrition and there is hunger. There is obesity. How do we bring these contradictions into focus? We need to start with the individual, continue with the family unit, the community and the nation as a whole. To people in other cultures or different economic positions, it may seem comical to consider the moral dilemma of a highly paid executive regretting having spent too little time with the family, or a celebrity complaining about lack of privacy. After all, those people seem to have it all. In their place, we wouldn't be complaining! However, the more access to material things people have, the more they tend to assign a higher value to the things that money can't buy. And here lies the difference between being rich and living richly. The two do not necessarily go together. The key to living richly is to be true to yourself. Know your dream, have faith that whatever you ask in prayer has already been granted, work diligently to make it happen, and share the fruits of success. It may very well be that your dream does not require the acquisition of wealth. Most commonly, the dream will be connected with some degree of material gain. Wealth is the means to reach the goal, not the goal in itself. Riches can only provide the pleasure that their possessors assign to them.

From the individual and the family unit, the next level in our social organization is our community. We can get a glimpse into the economic practices of the community in the early church in Acts 2 42:47. Believers shared everything with a sincere heart; they gave up their possessions and goods to help others in need. Such an organization is inconceivable in our 21st century capitalist economy. The idea of a common coffer may seem unattainable. The deep rift between those who have and those who have not is becoming painfully wider. It is a convenient way to ease our conscience to shrug off people on welfare thinking they got themselves into that situation because they are either lazy or prone to vice. Through my work with the underprivileged I have found that the opposite is mostly true. These people have limited skills and lacked the opportunity to catch up with the demands of our fast paced society. Before they can get up to speed, the gap has irretrievably widened beyond their reach. Every effort, every single achievement of those fortunate enough to enjoy economic success should strive to bring this gap closer together. A successful business must return to the community what the community gave to it, and more. It is ethical indeed to strive to succeed, to reach for the pinnacle of our occupation or field, as long as it is accompanied by an awakened social conscience and the actions that flow from there. Wealth reached through hard work, or a great idea, and shared with the community is a triumph of our society. Any advancement or advantage obtained through manipulation, deceit or avoidance of responsibility is loathsome and should ignite our most incensed moral indignation. In recent scandals that rocked the financial world, we were witnesses to the lowest of possible ethical standards. Financial data was manipulated to make corporate statements look better than the actual results merited. Different levels of corporate representatives (including several CEO's) as well as legal and accounting professionals succeeded for a while in creating a billion dollar bubble to outmaneuver the market, getting fat executive bonuses in the process. Investors were left powerless on the sidelines until the scheme imploded and the paper shredders couldn't work fast enough in an attempt to get rid of the evidence. In the wake of this storm lie thousands of honest, hardworking people, stripped of their investments or jobs. The sad lesson learned by these scandals provoked a wave of review of ethical standards, from executive benefits to a campaign funding reform bill. There is indeed a deeper, more disturbing lesson. These professionals broke the trust of the stakeholders of their business. They perceived themselves to be beyond right and wrong. In their misguided conduct they believed that the ethical values of the common man were not applicable to them. They are paying a dear price for their arrogance. They created a great deal of suffering, mistrust and resentment. These individuals had no inner moral compass. This is what I mean when I say that ethics start with the individual. There are no number of checks and controls that can effectively ensure moral behavior. The rules will certainly be stricter after these severe incidents. But time and habit will relax their enforcement, and loopholes will be found. These corporations would do better to find the right person for the job, rather than the right rules for the person. An executive with clear inner principles will not deviate from the chosen path, no matter how enticing the lure. Such a person would be aware that unethical actions have devastating consequences to the lives of others.

In a larger context, the same principles apply to the leaders of a nation. Being the world's wealthiest and most powerful country carries with it great responsibility, almost too much to bear. The destiny of millions is affected by the decisions of a handful of men and women. Let us pray that these chosen few are in possession of an incorruptible moral center, and that the Holy Spirit will enlighten and guide them during their mandate. We must remember that our powerful state once began as a rogue nation, tentatively asserting its position in world affairs. Over two centuries, our country took flight on the wings of free enterprise and entrepreneurial initiative. But these two elements alone could not have yielded the results that we enjoy today. There were other less desirable factors involved in our development, such as forced labor by indentured servants and slavery. Every hard earned breakthrough in this respect was the result of bitter racial and social struggles. We owe it to previous generations to preserve the great nation they helped build with their sweat and tears. We have been slowly moving away from God, love and justice, exchanging them for mere theories concerning supply and demand. Today, we have become the richest country in the world and in the process we have come to be perceived as wasteful and arrogant. I regret to admit that this ill reputation for the most part is well deserved. We are ravaging the world's supply of natural resources in a manner disproportionate to our numbers. We are always striving for the biggest and best of everything in painful disregard to our neighbors and the generations to come. Still, in the midst of this American cornucopia, people go to bed hungry every night.

I do believe that we are a nation with a big, open, giving heart. Whenever a charitable effort is attempted, the response is overwhelmingly generous. I believe that the Christian values that fueled the sacrifice and heroism of our forefathers have been inherited by our families, through our schools, our communities, and by the example provided by history for our business and political leaders to follow. If the leaders of our day would only show us the way, we are willing and ready to follow. They need to show us the way to a life of sharing wealth with other nations. They need to lead our efforts to conserve our planet's resources. Essentially, our Lord wants us as a nation to live more simply so that others may simply live.

9. Ethics and Pride

"When pride comes, then comes disgrace,
but with humility comes wisdom."
Proverbs 11:2

Pride. Is it a sin or a virtue? If we are to rely on cultural cues, we find the information confusing. It seems to be scattered in both directions.

Pride is often correlated with arrogance and selfish conceit. There seems to be a taboo on pride, considered as it is to be the root of all corruptions of the spirit. Calvin, in his Institutes of the Christian Religion, writes, "we cannot think of ourselves as we ought to think without utterly despising everything that may be supposed an excellence within us." This implies that the we should have nothing to be proud about ourselves. He even calls "self-love" a "pest". Kant follows basically the same attitude but differentiates between "self-love", a benevolence towards oneself, and "arrogance", the pleasure in oneself. He further proposes that the former must be restricted by ethical principles, while the latter must always be obliterated in order to retain a wholesome humility. Christianity has damned pride as one of the deadly sins. And yet in some passages of the Bible we find pride used under a different light, a benevolent light. In Isaiah 60:15 we get a sense for a kind of pride that is good in God's eyes "Although you have been forsaken and hated, with no one traveling through, I will make you the everlasting pride and the joy of all generations". In Proverbs 17:6 we can interpret pride as a reward" Children's children are a crown to the aged, and parents are the pride of their children." Aristotle proposed that "Pride, then, seems to be a sort of crown of the virtues; for it makes them greater, and it is not found without them." Could Aristotle be referring to the same thing? Is it possible then that there are different aspects of what we generally call pride? According to Aristotle, pride is a desirable emotion - one which results from healthy respect of oneself. It makes us wish to improve ourselves in order to keep feeling this pride. We need pride in order to be confident on our abilities and our capacity to face difficulties and overcome them. Pride is directly related to self-esteem and self-reliance to the point where the two cannot exist without a foundation of pride.

In order to clarify the role of pride in our Christian lives, let us make a distinction. The pride that is based in arrogance and conceit I will call "false pride", and I will give the name of "humble pride" to the healthy, God–inspired kind.

False pride is about positioning. We appoint ourselves as the judge of others, because we believe we are better, or know better. With this feeling of superiority, which can be conscious or unconscious, we find aspects in others that should be or shouldn't be and compare them with our own. Whenever we convince ourselves that other people are wrong, or when we attain something better, bigger or higher, our ego receives an emotional boost. Some people live constantly checking external references to make sure they are thin enough, rich enough, and handsome enough. They become so preoccupied in obtaining their own advantage that there is no room left for anything else. The motivation of every action is to look good to themselves and others. A voice goes on constantly in their heads, checking the shoulds and shouldn'ts to make sure that the image they project is one of success. Whenever these checks come back positive, they feel pride, if they don't they feel embarrassed or frustrated. This explains why tabloid news has such widespread appeal. So many people observe celebrities to see what they are wearing, buying, or saying. It is a known fact that these tabloids carry very little information and mostly rely on effect to feed entertainment to their hungry audience. Celebrities mostly play along, providing opportunities to look good in the public eye, or to appear controversial and provocative, depending on their target market. Celebrity watchers, however, translate this illusion into their own realities and sometimes tragically strive to reach these arbitrary standards. Fashion and culture dictate the guidelines. Even if people can temporarily keep up with these standards for success, they are based on an illusion, and sooner or later the illusion comes crashing down under them. This is likely to happen when a personal crisis forces the person to confront the emptiness that the ego based success brought with it. I know many people, too many unfortunately, that realize after their children have grown up and left the home that they did not spend enough time with their family because they were working so hard pursuing their careers. Until now, they had been proud of their achievements. But they had been building their lives on empty goals, imposed by external images. I have seen marriages fall apart because one partner needed to affirm a sense of self, and chooses to do so with a new younger person in a vain attempt to reclaim the treasures of youth. These people have anchored their self-esteem around an external system of benchmarks. But these benchmarks are built on very soft sand, and the anchor does not hold. The basic relationship with others is that of competition, governed by the forces of the market. When the goals do not satisfy the ego anymore, people are eager to submit to a new set of rules as long as they stay in the game. The new ideals are equally elusive. False pride keeps the mind in disquiet and uneasiness. There is an underlying spirit of distrust and hostility to others. We often wonder why people who seem to have everything suddenly break down and fall deep into darkness. Or we feel puzzled at why apparently successful individuals decide one day to end their lives. According to our standards, these people should have been feeling high at the top of their self-esteem scale. But inside them, the illusion shattered and they were left with an image of themselves they could not feel proud of anymore. The illusion now failed to sustain them. False pride is an ailment of the soul; in the long run it only brings misery and pain.

Although it may seem at first glance that pride and humility don't go together, I believe they do. In fact, pride achieves its ethical manifestation only when it is accompanied by the antidote of humility. I am not proposing a reevaluation of our values, but that we identify them in their true nature. It is important that humility not come from a sense of resignation, giving up on the pressures of society and possibly holding a grudge for not reaching the goals set out for us by external factors. It is not a defiance to society and its values. Humility in its spiritual sense comes entirely from within, and does not need validation from anything or anyone outside of ourselves. Would it be surprising to find that we cannot love others if we do not love ourselves first? Propaganda techniques have taken advantage of the notion that love of self and love of others are mutually exclusive. The Nazi organization, for example, drove forth the banner that public good takes precedence over private good. They aimed at molding a society of guilt-ridden individuals who only lived for relentless work and felt worthless otherwise. This doctrine controls people by eliminating their individuality. But man has a basic desire to wish things for himself. We can see it openly in children, before their behavior is modified by their environment. Young children have a natural inclination to satisfy their own desires. The child's character will be tempered by the ethical values imbued by the family, school and society. These principles guide our character to look less for ourselves and more to love others. But if it is a virtue to love others, does it not then follow that I must love myself as well? Can I profess solidarity and charity without including myself in them too? This is perhaps the root of the confusion regarding the applicability of humble pride. When we say to our children: "Don't be selfish"; do we really mean "Don't love yourself: or Don't respect yourself"? I doubt it. Rather, we are trying to instill humility and selflessness. We are asking them not to be arrogant or conceited. It would not be healthy to ask for complete submission, or total renunciation of any desire the child might have. What we are attempting to develop is the child's inner ethical guide, such as will produce feelings of pride in the satisfaction of a job well done, or in the contentment of a good deed done for another, without need of external validation. Such is the inner glow of humble pride. Pride is a matter of giving our personal best. The love for ourselves and our love for others, far from being contradictory, run closely linked together. Many of us adopt a feeling that we know we are supposed to have: to like others, to be nice to others. This feeling has a thinness to it, more like compensation than sincere fondness. It almost implies that people are not really likeable and we need to make an effort to overcome this basic state of "unlove". Other people, on the opposite side of the scale, feel that they are not good enough to be liked by others. Their basic lack of fondness for their own person affects their perception of the world. They may feel unattractive, awkward or stupid. They tend to withdraw or hide their insecurity behind a veil of hostility. There is a third group that mostly likes themselves and finds others rather tolerable, but whenever they find fault with themselves or others their criticism spins out of proportion. Their love does not allow for any mistakes. But in a state of unconditional love, we are all free and equal. We rest comfortably within ourselves, without anxiety or comparison. This is what Jesus teaches as the greatest commandment: to love God with all our hearts, and to love others as ourselves. To God, we are all at once equal and unique. Each and every individual has the capacity for excellence, in its own unique manifestation. In our human limitation, some achievements may seem to us more excellent than others. Some types of excellence are easier to recognize. Few would disagree with the statement that Mozart was an excellent composer of music. He left behind an amazing collection of work that continues to uplift us and bring joy to listeners centuries after his death. This must certainly be an achievement a person can be rightfully proud of. If we look around us, to the people we come in contact with daily, not many of us can claim a talent equivalent to Mozart's, even if we expand our search to other fields and not limit our search to music. But the truth is that we all have the potential for excellence, it lies in our ability to give our absolute best. Once we let the love of God into our hearts we are then able to project this love outside of ourselves to all of humanity. We begin to see excellence in each one of us. I am amazed at some people's ability to speak words of kindness where they are needed. In difficult situations where others would stumble to find an awkward word of encouragement, their voice rings with sympathy and hope. There are people who are amazing parents. They naturally seem to find the right decision in every situation and they thrive in the challenges of raising a family. There are people who can make a difficult job seem simple, and people who can see humor in the testiest of situations. It is not easy to describe what these people have, except to say that there is an excellence about them. There are so many different kinds of excellence, not just the kind that deserves world recognition or a lifetime achievement award. Most of the people I have just described live out their excellence in all humility. Could we honestly believe that it would be wrong of them to feel proud of their particular brand of special talents? Humble pride is an appreciation of our own personal best. It is an expression of our love for ourselves. This love is indivisible. It is one love, embracing God, ourselves and others. In the affirmation of this love, any external goal falls in its proper place, in relation with the deeper meaning held by being a witness of God's creation. In this state of grace, our pride is humble and thankful. We are proud to live according to Jesus' teachings, and to follow him in His path of light. Pride originates from our fundamental desire to improve ourselves. Humble pride builds strong, God-inspired self-confidence, necessary to endure the inevitable storms of life and ultimately see us through them. We should always be watchful of our pride, and make sure that it is tempered with humility. Whenever we are able to feel and show our love for others, a smile bursting inside our spirit, our humble pride will warm our hearts and give us a sense of renewed hope.

The self-esteem movement has perhaps abused the term pride as the prevailing theme to exalt the worship of self. Culture, however, is modifiable by human endeavors. Culture and custom are human constructions, and as such can be both challenged and perfected. It is dangerous to reject our culture and condemn it as evil, or to withdraw into our own self-righteousness. As Christians we need to come to terms with our world, embrace all that is good in it, and make better anything that needs to be changed… and be humbly proud of our achievement.

10. Ethics and Power

"Nearly all men can stand adversity, but if you want to test
a man's character, give him power."
Abraham Lincoln

There is a common misconception as to the idea of power. Power corrupts. Power leaves loss and suffering in its wake. I would like to make a distinction between this type of power, which is certainly a reality, and the power that generates good and promotes healing and harmony.

We can think of the different types of power as to the manner in which it is achieved. There are as many different ways to come into power as the imagination can produce. I will pick a few examples in order to illustrate the discussion.

Let me define for a moment what I mean by power, or rather what I don't. I am not discussing here any type of physical, psychic, athletic or mental power. I am in fact referring to power as the control or influence over others.

One way of access is by the voluntary delegation of power on the part of a group of people. Such is the power of Presidents and Prime Ministers elected by popular vote. Such is also the power of the Captain of a team that has been elected by its members. The appointment to such a position of power gives the elected person access to decide on the fate of others, and to influence and control their actions. There are different degrees of power and there are opposed and balancing forces to counteract any potential abuse. In the absence of such a balancing force, the holder of these powers can rapidly veer off the intended course into autocratic power. Such is the case of a dictatorship, as in the recent example of Saddam Hussein in Iraq, or Adolph Hitler during the Second World War.

It also holds true that a leader cannot be effective without power. A Captain of a ship who has formal authority but no power over his officers and crew will not be able to run an efficient operation. The Captain, in times of emergency, needs to elicit immediate and unhesitating obedience. Should he allow his power to be questioned or doubted, he would in fact be putting the lives of his crew in danger. The Captain's power does not automatically arise from his appointment. That is only the formal power he will possess. He will be observed closely and most probably challenged at some point. His qualifications and knowledge will play a part in earning his actual power, but his own conduct and the way he interacts with his crew will become the critical factor.

Power can also be inherited, acquired by the accumulation of wealth, or gained by a million different methods. Whichever its form, however, there is a universal truth to which I wholeheartedly subscribe to: power cannot corrupt a moral man. The fringe benefits that power can bring with it can create a mirage around the holder. Suddenly this person has access to things and places he never had before. An order given transforms into action. Power often attracts an inner circle of servile people who flood their leader with flattery and adulation. The effect can be intoxicating. Examples are around us in abundance, I am sad to say. A large number of SS officers in the Nazi regime were men of moderate or limited capacity who were given far reaching powers and expected to return blind loyalty to their leader. The savage effects of putting these mediocre men in control of the destinies of helpless millions is painfully known to us today.

Power is also generated by fear. Let me give you an example that is closer to home. The Internal Revenue Service wills a tremendous source of power through its ability to put fear into the minds of individuals and business owners who have not fulfilled their obligations punctually. Many of these people are stressed out to the limit. They are not trying to defraud the government; it is simply that they do not have the ability to pay. The corporate giant has a powerful legal department to obtain relief on their tax obligations. This is their opposing force. The small business owner or individual taxpayer has no access to such resources and is therefore subject to the fear of losing his business or his property. The mere notice of an audit throws this person into a world of despair. So it is a fact that the big corporation has a better chance of getting out of these situations unscathed. Ethical? Ethics and taxes are rarely seen dancing together.

The sources of power that we have discussed so far all come from circumstances external to the individual (an election, fear, wealth). There are legitimate sources of power that well up from within.

Prestige, for example, is a source of intrinsic power. It comes in the way you project yourself and in the way others perceive you. It is accumulated over the course of time, and it is the kind of power that grows stronger as we age. An academic, for example, builds on his prestige as one of his most valuable career assets. Through the publication of his work, the recognition from his peers and pertinent academic organizations, he collects the building blocks of his prestige. His ethical conduct (or at least the appearance of it) is a major component of his prestige. As his prestige grows, so does his power. Once he has gained recognition as an authority in his field, he will be able to influence others through his work. Imagine this academic trying to publish an innovative idea when he is fresh out of his Ph.D. dissertation. Now imagine the same scholar, presenting the very same idea for publication after he has just been awarded the Nobel Prize in the field. Clearly, he will have a greater power to influence the publisher's decision in the second instance.

Then there is latent power. This kind of power is found in most men and women. It is not frequently used. The reason is that the holder of this power does not realize that they have it until an emergency arises and they are called to action against their will. This power responds when challenged, and otherwise lays dormant. Oppression and injustice often give birth to unlikely leaders. Meek people who had no aspirations to leadership are suddenly thrown into the battle and come out ahead, powerful and proud. Adversity can awaken the power that is latent within us. This power can erupt with great force, and wash away anything that stands in its way. Power is not evil or good in itself. It is just the way we use it that makes the difference. As long as we are aware of our own power, whatever its subtle degree and whatever its source, we can channel it to fall towards its most ethical and moral applications.

It is only within the moral fiber of the individual that the fine balance of power is struck. A person with firm inner principles has a clear distinction between using the power for the purpose it has been gained, and using it merely as a means to an end. The morally powerful person will know what is right and what is true. In contrast, no amount of external checks and balances will prevent an immoral leader from abusing his privileges. It is therefore imperative that a society elect its leaders based on their ethical track record. Once the leader is in power, the lack of ethical reasoning will become only more dangerous to society. Ethical leaders will weigh their decisions taking into account their duty to society rather than the effect of the decision on opinion polls.

Absolute power bestows upon the holder the ability to work one's will against all opposition. At some point in our lives, all of us have access to this power, if only for a brief moment or an isolated occasion. What we do with such power reveals more about ourselves than we would like to admit. Take for example the power that a parent has over an infant. The parent is infinitely more powerful than the child. This is not only true physically, but there is also power in the ability to withdraw food, entertainment or even affection. When the child becomes irritating and the parent's patience is severely tested, then is the time for the ethics of power to be revealed. Is the parent aware, at all times, of his or her infinitely superior power in respect to the child? Can the parent practice temperance, and wisdom without giving in to the temptation to abuse his power to stop the undesired conduct? Any of you who have raised children will agree that there are times when this fine line becomes very blurred. This is an example that we can observe on a daily basis, but there are innumerable subtle power struggles at work in politics, in business, and certainly in the church. The underlying principle, however, is the same. The power we come into should be used for the benefit of those who have bestowed it on us. The power that we seek solely inspired by greed or ambition will turn back against us and corrupt our integrity.

Finally, I am happy to point out; there is power in ethics. The holder of power in possession of a strong ethical backbone will be ennobled by such power and will rise above corruption. The leader who scores high on the ethical scale will only see his power augmented even more, as he increases in prestige and in the respect from his followers.

Earthly power is transitory. It is easier to measure power in hindsight. The history of the great empires reveals that there is a cyclical pattern to great power: Roman, Ottoman, Napoleonic, British and eventually American. They rise, they rule and they eventually decline. On a micro level, there also are cycles that flow up, down and into each other. The life of a person is a cycle. A baby is powerless and depends on his parents for survival. As the child grows into adulthood, it defines itself separately from the parents and grows into a power of its own. Upon reaching old age, a person again is dependent on others for the simplest tasks of daily life, almost akin to becoming a child again. In most societies, the family unit is the fabric that holds all these cycles together. The relatively more powerful adults take care of the children and the elderly, until eventually it will be their turn to receive that care. In a developed nation, the active labor force contributes to the maintenance of those who have retired. We live in a world where power is a tangible reality. It is a world of action. And a world of reaction. The wheels of power never stop spinning, reflecting the ebb and flow of the great mystery of our lives on earth. Any attempt to make it permanent is futile. And any time that power is relinquished there is someone or something else, ready to take it away. Power sets wheels in motion that are not easy to stop. In this respect, as a powerful and wealthy nation, it is our duty and our responsibility to the rest of the world to use our power wisely, with measure, and in harmony with a solid moral compass.

There is but one form of permanent, transcendental power, and this is the power of the Lord. The power of men will pass and fade but the Word of God will stand forever. His power is absolute. This power comes through as evident as ever in Mark 8:31 "he then began to teach them that the Son of Man must suffer many things and be rejected by the elders, chief priests and teachers of the law, and that he must be killed and after three days rise again." Jesus not only described what would happen. He knew that he would be ridiculed, tortured and killed. The only way he could get through such an ordeal was to intimately know the absolute, infinite power of his Father. He would rise again. And so He did, as we know from Mark 16:1-19, three days later, on Easter Sunday. His power is such that he can forecast it, and it will happen just as He said. And so it didn't matter if He was humiliated and put through excruciating pain. He would rise again. And so it is for us, just the same. His love for us is such that he puts this power at our disposal. He sends us the Holy Spirit, so that we can summon its power to carry out God's work in His name. I have seen the Lord's power at work, in my life and in the lives of many others. I am in awe of this power, and I have devoted my life to sharing the good news with others. I have traveled the world carrying His message. I braved adversity and His power carried me through my own resurrections. I hope that at the end of this book, you too, will receive His message. I hope I can provide you with sufficient structure for you to bring this message into your life, and experience for yourself the utmost power we will ever know, the power of our Lord.

11. Restorative Justice

"It is not good to be partial to the wicked,
or to deprive the innocent of justice."
Proverbs 18:5

Restorative justice is the term widely used to describe a philosophical approach about how society should respond to crimes and other anti-social behavior. In general terms, this philosophy supports the development of methods that encourage offenders to understand the consequences of their behavior and make amends for their actions. In contrast, the philosophy of retributive justice advocates the punishment of the offender; and provides that such punishment is to be decided by an independent authority.

Although we largely associate *restorative justice* with its practice in the field of criminal justice, it is not a specific program, but rather a way of thinking about how society responds to problematic situations. It is a set of values that can guide decisions in multiple areas such as discipline in school settings, healing wounds within a faith community, civil disputes, or problems between neighbors, to name a few. For the purposes of our discussion, we will omit any consideration to retributive justice since the concept falls under the jurisdiction of the judicial system, and address the implications of restorative justice in the realm of ethical conflict.

First let me say that, after giving the matter careful consideration, I believe that there is no such thing as a victimless ethical offense. By the nature of the act, the ethical offense involves a violation of a relationship or a breach of trust, regardless of the extent of the harm caused. Humans are capable of monstrous actions, denying that fact would be ignoring the reality of our very nature. Would it be enough for the offender to apologize, and move on? The Bible tells us to repent in order to atone for our sins. By confessing our sins and requesting forgiveness we restore our relationship with God. It is certainly right and necessary to repent in our hearts and confess with our voice. But if we stopped at repentance, we would not be taking the victim (or society) into consideration. Let me tell you about Amy and how she became the victim of blatant unethical conduct.

Amy is a paralegal in one of the most prestigious law firms in Washington, D.C. The firm deals with international law and their long standing prestige and reputation is their most valuable asset. As such, they are very cautious not only to keep up the practice of ethics but also to preserve the appearance of ethicality. There was an opportunity for a very desirable promotion coming up and three candidates were being considered. One of them was Amy. The other two candidates, Kevin and Adam, were slightly irritated that Amy was in the running since she was much younger and had worked for the company for a shorter time. One day, Adam casually dropped a comment in a water-cooler conversation. He said that he thought he might have seen Amy on a date out in the town with one of the firm's high-profile clients. Adam brazenly retold the details but said that it was dark, and, of course, he could be wrong. He asked his listener not to say a word of it because it would hurt Amy's career. Needless to say, Adam had never seen Amy; he was making the whole story up in the hope that it would taint Amy's candidacy for the coveted post. Adam had no intention of harming Amy personally, he just wanted to eliminate his competition. In fact, he regretted making the comment shortly after, but the damage was irreparably done. The malicious rumor made its way at lightning speed all the way to the Human Resources Manager. Because of Amy's sensitive position in the firm, it would be expected of her to disclose any personal involvement with a client of the firm. The Human Resources Manager had no way of proving that Amy had in fact any attachment of this nature, and could hardly bring up the subject at a higher level on the basis of office gossip since it would reflect badly on her. It was far easier for her to just drop Amy's name from the list of candidates based on Amy's short time with the firm, and move on. Amy had worked very hard at her job, and was by far the brightest and most qualified candidate for the promotion. She was doubly motivated to succeed because with the additional income she was planning to cover her younger brother's college expenses. She was crushed when the job went to Adam, but she gathered her spirits and sent him an email offering her congratulations. A few days later, Kevin, the other candidate who did not get the job, went up to Amy to commiserate on their rotten luck.

With his best intentions he told Amy that he had heard that her chances had been compromised by her dating a client without disclosing it. Amy could not believe her ears. Who could be so cruel as to make up such a vicious lie? She went home feeling depressed. She kept thinking that her younger brother would be deprived of his opportunity to go to college, an indirect victim of office gossip…

Restorative justice brings into play the concept of reparation. The primary aim of a restorative approach is to assess the extent of the harm, and to identify how that harm might be repaired. It seeks to engage offenders to enable them to understand the damage that they have caused, and to awaken in them the sense of obligation to make good. In contrast, punishment is a penalty inflicted for the sake of the penalty itself. Reparation, while still holding the offenders accountable, offers them the opportunity to take responsibility for their actions and make amends, as far as possible. This approach empowers the victim, who has a say in how the damage can be repaired. Any action to be taken by the offender to repair the damage must be mutually agreed, never imposed on the victim. Reparation can be made in numerous ways. Some examples of this are: a verbal or written apology, material compensation, or work carried out for the victim or a third party. The latter particularly applies when the victim is no longer in the picture. It may very well be that the victim has no desire to neither seek nor accept reparation, or does not wish to have any contact with the offender. In this case there is still opportunity for the offender to provide indirect reparation to the community, by way of a mutually agreed positive action that generates a good and desired effect. The question is, of course, what is the adequate reparation that fits the offense. In cases where there is material damage to property, for example, the damage may be relatively simple to identify and even to rectify. An ethical breach, however, often deals with emotions and human vulnerabilities (in addition to any physical or material damage inflicted). Any unilateral attempt to quantify the extent of the harm will probably fail. It is imperative that the victim be involved in defining both the harm and in identifying how that harm can be repaired. If, however, the victim cannot be reached or does not wish to be further involved with the offender, or has passed away, the offender must seek ways to do good for someone else, having been motivated by the need to make amends.

Going back to our example, when Adam received the congratulations from Amy, it made him very uncomfortable. He was glad to get the promotion, yet he couldn't fully enjoy it with this weight on his conscience. But now that the harm was already done, he didn't see any benefit in coming out with the truth and risk his own position. And yet, he was not the type to keep his mouth under control. So one day when he felt particularly remorseful, he approached Kevin, and confessed his guilt. Kevin asked him what he was planning to do about it. Adam said he was planning to do nothing, of course. There was no point in stirring up the whole thing again. Kevin told Adam very firmly, that if he didn't go to Amy and offer his apology, he and Adam could not continue to be friends. He explained to Adam the severity of what he had done, and made him appreciate how much it had hurt Amy. As a result of his conversation with Kevin, Adam gathered his courage and talked to Amy. Whereas Adam now felt somewhat relieved by the disclosure, the apology did nothing to improve Amy's situation. Realizing that some positive action on his part was necessary, Adam offered to write a letter to Human Resources to explain the "misunderstanding". But Amy strongly objected and asked Adam please not to do it, as that would only cause her more embarrassment. She had never been officially nominated for the promotion, and it would be presumptuous on her part to take it for granted, although she knew that her superior qualifications would have most likely caused her to be selected for the position. In any case, the firm would be unlikely to revert the decision and it would make everybody involved even more uncomfortable. But Amy did tell Adam that her real regret was that her brother would not get his education, at least not in the near future. And then Adam had an idea. He started doing research and helped Amy fill in applications for scholarships and financial aid. Although reluctant at first to deal with Adam in any capacity, Amy did recognize that he had a point, and that she should at least try all possible avenues before giving up on her brother. Adam made phone calls and networked to find out any information that could help Amy, and sent her a daily message with his progress. One of the leads proved useful and Amy was able to secure at least a partial scholarship for her brother's tuition expenses. She was now much closer to her goal, and she felt like something good had come out of all the aggravation.

Restorative Justice also incorporates the concept of reintegration. The objective of reintegration is to enable the offender to be regarded as a normal member of the community again. Associated with this is the belief that people who have offended will be at a disadvantage if they feel that they are regarded by those close to them, and by society, as worthless offenders. The aim of a restorative approach is to reestablish the offender's relationship with the victim in particular and with society as a whole. One way to effect this reintegration is through the action of a group of people that cares about the offender getting together and showing that they disapprove of his or her actions. The aim is to confront the offender with the consequences of the offense, and hold the offender accountable. In order to achieve its intended purpose, however, any criticism must be done in a supportive context to enable the offender to atone for the offense and thus to regain his status in the community.

Kevin enabled the restorative process by forcefully confronting Adam with the need to apologize to Amy. Had he made Adam feel like an outcast instead, or if Adam had been to proud and arrogant to want to make amends, the situation would have probably remained stagnant and the relationships would have been irreparably broken. In our example, while Amy never fully forgot Adam's wrongdoing towards her, she did reconcile with Adam, and the camaraderie in the office was restored. The three of them were able to share a productive working relationship. At this point we need to make a distinction between reparation and reconciliation, since the latter is entirely up to the victim. We find a good example of forgiveness and reconciliation in the story of Joseph's dreams (Genesis 37-50).

Joseph lived in Canaan with his father and his eleven brothers. His brothers were jealous of him because his father favored Joseph over the rest. One day when they were out in the fields, they saw the opportunity to make some money and get rid of Joseph at the same time: they sold him as a slave. When they got back home, they presented evidence to their elderly father to lead him to believe that Joseph had been the victim of an attack by a wild animal. Joseph was taken to Egypt where he suffered years of imprisonment and humiliation. He had the gift of divination, and word of these powers got to Pharaoh, the head of state. By interpreting Pharaoh's dreams Joseph was able to warn him of an impending famine in time to stock up on grain and supplies, thereby allowing Egypt to survive the peril. Pharaoh made Joseph his minister and put him in charge of the whole of Egypt. In this way, after years of heartbreak and suffering, Joseph was suddenly powerful and wealthy. By this time the famine had reached Canaan, and Joseph's brothers embarked on a journey to Egypt to buy grain because they had heard that there was enough food there. They were taken before Joseph. He recognized his brothers but they did not recognize him. They bowed and paid their respects to him. At this point Joseph had his brothers, who had wronged him so deeply, entirely at his mercy. When he made himself known to them, they were terrified. They threw themselves down before him begging for mercy. Joseph chose forgiveness instead of revenge, and spoke kindly to them. He reassured them and instructed them to bring back their entire family to Egypt where they would be provided for. Joseph knew in his heart that it was not up to him, but to God, to exact justice over their actions. It was sufficient for him to know that they had changed for the better. We find the same message from St. Paul's in his letter to the Romans "Do not repay anyone evil for evil" (Romans, 12:19).

In conclusion, the act of repentance as evidenced by sincere contrition and acknowledgement of the wrongdoing is only the first step. Remorse must be followed by a resolve to cease the wrongdoing and return to the right action by restitution. Communities have an invaluable role in demanding accountability and in enabling the reparation and reintegration process. It is up to each of us, as followers of Jesus Christ, to find forgiveness and reconciliation in our hearts and thus exemplify restorative justice in its most positive form.

12. Ethics and War

"When the rich wage war, it's the poor who die"
Jean-Paul Sartre

The purpose of war ethics is to decide what is right or wrong about war, both for individuals and countries. It is also helpful to guide decisions in public policy and government. Whenever I refer to war, I include both civil and national wars, declared publicly or by action. More than an act, war is a condition in which nations involved in a dispute or controversy decide to use force to resolve the outcome. Some wars have followed a formal declaration, and others have been started de facto. Many wars have been fought by armed forces in uniform, such as World War II, and yet many others are carried out with less obvious identification of the opposing factions, as in the case of guerilla warfare.

In any discussion about war and ethics we need to address a basic underlying question: Is it ever right to go to war? Mankind has been engaged in fighting since the beginning of time. For just as long, this question has generated controversy and occupied the minds of great philosophers and theologians alike, in an attempt to reconcile the precept that the taking of human life is wrong with the need to defend innocent lives and important moral values. The mainstream ideology on war has changed over time, including the views of Christianity on the matter. Whatever the school of thought, however, they all agree on the basic principle that war is bad, and should be avoided if possible.

People who object to war may do so based on different beliefs:

- Their religious beliefs
- Their human-rights beliefs or non-religious beliefs in the preservation of human life
- Their practical belief that war is not an effective way to resolve conflicts

Pacifism is one of the philosophies that oppose war. There are different levels of pacifism, but in essence they all maintain that violence is never justified, and conflicts should be settled in a peaceful way. The most extreme pacifist believes that the use of violence is never justified, not even in self-defense or to protect an innocent person who is being attacked. The moderate pacifist believes that there are instances in which war may be unavoidable, but they object to certain methods of warfare, such as nuclear or biological weapons because of their devastating effects. Based on these beliefs, many pacifists will refuse to fight during a war, or they will play a non-combative role; e.g. as clerks, reporters, drivers, cooks or laborers. The argument against pacifism is that any nation that would undertake such policy would result in that nation sitting vulnerable to being attacked or conquered by non-pacifist enemies. Those who oppose pacifism maintain that since the world is not perfect, there will always be war, and anybody who refuses to participate in a war is failing to carry out an important moral obligation to his or her country. The concept of pacifism, however, does play a weighty role in politics in the quest for peaceful resolution to international conflicts, as evidenced by the formation of organizations such as the United Nations.

Non-violence is another philosophy that opposes the use of force. It does not stop at just not committing violent acts, but also includes taking positive action against injustice or to effect change. One of the staunchest upholders of non-violence was Mohandas Gandhi, who led the opposition of India to British rule in the 20th century. Gandhi said that the essence of the non-violent technique is that it seeks to liquidate antagonisms but not the antagonist. He also made it clear that it was not a tool for cowards to hide behind, because he considered non-violence to be a weapon of the strong. Some examples of non-violent actions are:

- hunger strikes
- sit-ins
- vigils
- civil disobedience (such as not saluting a flag)

Some religions such as Buddhism contain strong pacifist elements. Judaism is strongly opposed to violence and where violence is permitted it limits its use to the minimum extent necessary. For many centuries Christians viewed the use of violence as right and proper - the Crusades constitute a prime example. In the Christian tradition, St. Augustine in the 4th Century stated that "we do not seek peace in order to be at war, but we go to war that we may have peace." He maintained that war is justifiable if its intention is doing good. This position is similar to Aristotle's claim that "We make war that we may live in peace". The weakness of this argument is, of course, that it is illogical to attempt to make the world less violent by using violence as a tool. Or as the popular saying goes - *you can't dig yourself out of a hole*. St. Thomas Aquinas in the 13th century took St. Augustine's philosophy one step further and added the requirement that a justifiable war needed to be legally sanctioned. This early doctrine developed into what we now know as the Doctrine of the Just War, adopted by various denominations of Christianity, which is summarized by the Catholic Church as follows:

"The strict conditions for legitimate defense by military force require rigorous consideration. The gravity of such a decision makes it subject to rigorous conditions of moral legitimacy. At one and the same time:

The damage inflicted by the aggressor on the nation or community of nations must be lasting, grave, and certain;

All other means of putting an end to it must have been shown to be impractical or ineffective;

There must be serious prospects of success;

The use of arms must not produce evils and disorders graver than the evil to be eliminated. The power of modern means of destruction weighs very heavily in evaluating this condition.

These are the traditional elements enumerated in what is called the 'just war' doctrine. The evaluation of these conditions for moral legitimacy belongs to the prudential judgment of those who have responsibility for the common good." (from the Catechism of the Catholic Church).

From this doctrine we derive that although the aim of Christianity is to promote peace and justice in the world, war may sometimes be necessary as the lesser of all evils, a lesser injustice than tolerating the victimization of innocent people or aberrations of important moral values. It is a continuation of the idea of violence as a tool to restore justice and peace. There are obvious difficulties in the application of this doctrine to actual conflicts such as to determine what is just cause, and what constitutes a reasonable chance of success. It occurs to me that the people in charge of deliberating about and ultimately declaring war, are removed from any danger of being involved in the fighting themselves. I often wonder what would be their position if the first line of fire was formed by their own sons and daughters. I hold people in the highest esteem who have conscientiously served in the armed forces. They have received the call of a human institution they love and respect, and responded to that call with honor. As Christians we are urged to do so in 1 Peter 2:13 "Submit yourselves for the Lord's sake to every authority instituted among men..." It is in the words of one of such men that I found the most eloquent opposition to war. General Douglas Macarthur, the most decorated American soldier of the First World War and one of the most hallowed heroes of W.W. II said, "I knew war as few other men now living know it, and nothing to me is more revolting. I have long advocated its complete abolition, as its very destructiveness on both friend and foe has rendered it useless as a method of settling international disputes." War spells incalculable loss to both victor and vanquished. Any war, however victorious to one side, is a defeat to humanity. Time after time, wars have engendered fresh resentment and spawned new conflict. World War II was dubbed the "War to End All Wars". Since then, we have witnessed major conflicts such as Korea, Vietnam, Iraq, Bosnia, Afghanistan and so many other violent civil and international confrontations.

It is not, however, my intention to focus on the political or secular tenets of war ethics. It is my one guiding objective to follow Jesus, both his teachings and his example. I seek, therefore, to shed light on the question of the right or wrong of war by looking to Jesus Christ for guidance. In the Bible, we find a contrast between the treatment of the subject of war in the Old Testament and the New. In the Old Testament, war almost always refers to armed conflict between nations. War was in some respects a religious act. Israel was both a people of God and a nation, and as such it was subject to the political, social and economic struggles that were common to all nations. In the New Testament, war more often refers to spiritual conflict against evil. Unlike Israel, the church is no longer one of the nations of the world; rather it is transnational, composed of peoples from all nations. Warfare is not against enemies of flesh and blood but rather against the forces of evil bent on destroying God's work; it follows that the defense must therefore be spiritual. The Apostle Paul writes in his letter to the Ephesians (6:11-17) "Put on the full armor of God so that you can take your stand against the devil's schemes. For our struggle is not against flesh and blood, but against the rulers, the authorities, against the powers of this dark world and against the spiritual forces of evil in the heavenly realms. Therefore put on the full armor of God, so that when the day of evil comes, you may be able to stand your ground, and after you have done everything, to stand. Stand firm then, with the belt of truth buckled around your waist, with the breastplate of righteousness in place and with your feet fitted with the readiness that comes from the gospel of peace. In addition to all this, take up the shield of faith, with which you can extinguish all the flaming arrows of the evil one. Take the helmet of salvation and the sword of the Spirit which is the word of God." So this is the war we are meant to wage, and these are the weapons we are meant to brandish. Jesus did not command his disciples to use warfare as a means of conquest. He seems to have rejected any implication that he was the leader of a war to restore the Kingdom of Israel "Jesus, knowing that they intended to come and make him King by force, withdrew again to a mountain by himself" (John 6:15). Jesus said to Pilate "My Kingdom is not of this world. If it were, my servants would fight to prevent my arrest by the Jews. But now my kingdom is from another place" (John 18:36). It is clear to me that Jesus did not lead us to warring our fellow men, and even rebuked a disciple who used a sword to protect Him from the people who had come to arrest Him "Put your sword back in its place", Jesus said to him, "for all who draw the sword will die by the sword". (Matthew 26:52). But the most poignant event in the teachings of Jesus is found in the Beatitudes. I believe that Jesus meant exactly what he said, and that when he speaks to us, he is giving us clear directions on how to lead our lives: "Blessed are the peacemakers, for they will be called sons of God" (Mathew 5:9). As a follower of Jesus it is therefore unthinkable to support the deliberate killing of people. His teachings are not easy to follow, or pleasant to comply with: "Love your enemies, do good to those who hate you, bless those who curse you, pray for those who mistreat you"(Luke 6:27). "Be merciful, just as your Father is merciful" (Luke 6:36)

Jesus' teachings and His example are meant for us to be followed in order to do what is right in the eyes of the Lord. In the face of this clear set of instructions, how could we possible justify the taking of even one life? Even in those instances in which war may be deemed the lesser of all evils, it is still an evil. War is fundamentally wrong. In war there is sin. In war there is despair, chaos, suffering and death. There are no winners, only greater or lesser losers. Let us not claim, therefore, that we go to war as Christians, but rather, if faced with no choice, that we go to war with sadness in our hearts as men and women following the command of the leaders of our nation. I do not know if I will ever see an end to war in my lifetime. I pray to God that the leaders of the nations of this world will find guidance in their hearts to accomplish the resolution of their differences by non-violent means. I offer my most fervent prayer that the words of Isaiah 2:4 come true for mankind; "they will beat their swords into ploughshares and their spears into pruning hooks. Nation will not take up sword against nation, nor will they train for war anymore".

13. Ethics in the Media

"I find television very educating. Every time somebody turns the set on, I go into the other room and read a book."
Groucho Marx

Most of what we learn about people and the world around us comes less from personal experience than from mass-circulation media such as television, film, radio, books, magazines, newspapers and the internet. In many countries, the media is regulated by the government. In the United States, however, we believe that a free media is at the heart of a free society and therefore rely on market forces, competition, responsibility and a set of self-controls to provide an ethical framework for the fulfillment of their mission. The need for a set of ethical principles in the media is the same as the need for ethical principles in society as a whole. They define accepted behavior, promote high standards of practice and establish a guideline for self-evaluation. In the media, in particular, a high code of ethics enhances a sense of community among its members, and a sense of pride in belonging to a profession with common values and a common mission.

No set of guidelines can establish principles to govern every possible situation. Common sense and judgment are to be applied to the realities of every day work. Each publication or broadcasting entity should further develop the general guidelines into particular policies that apply specifically to their own situation, as well as the manner in which these guidelines are to be enforced.

It is natural for us, in the case of a breach of ethics by a journalist or editor, to assume that the person responsible for the article should be held accountable for the consequences of that breach. However, this assumes that the journalist is relatively independent, or free to make decisions associated with his or her job without outside pressure or influence. Under normal circumstances, we assume that media practitioners have autonomy. However, the nature of the pressures under which journalists work today has changed. The most implacable and troubling influences in all forms of media now come from the inside. The temptation to avoid responsibility on moral decisions increases (and becomes easier) as the organizational hierarchy becomes more complex. Media are becoming big business. Newspapers are owned by huge corporate holdings, public relations and advertising are often partners under the same umbrella. The lines of ownership are blurred. The entertainment function often overrides the information function. Accountability is spread thin throughout large and complex organizations. Complex organizations tend toward decentralized decision-making which calls decision makers at different levels of the organization. The ideal would be for both the decision making power and the accountability of the decision making to fall on the same person. Mostly, this is not the case. In present day organizations, it is increasingly easy to dilute accountability in the multiple layers of decision-making. Moral evasion becomes the rule rather than the exception. It is too easy to blame others for decisions over which we have had minimal input or control. This failure to assume accountability for our actions because of orders from above is becoming more frequent. Some business journalists are mystified as to why people make such a fuss about investing in the industries they are covering. They even act as consultants for the same companies they review. They are so inter-related with the people they are supposed to cover that they don't even realize that it in order to maintain a reporter's perspective they need to maintain an arm's length relationship. Or they are simply following orders from somebody who is in turn following orders who in turn is not quite sure where the original orders actually originate. What is a journalist to do when trying to impartially report some damaging news about a company owned by the same conglomerate as his employer?

The principle of freedom of the press is one worth upholding with all our might. It is perhaps, the one constitutional mandate that ensures democracy over any other. However, those who are genuinely concerned in protecting the integrity of the First Amendment, and the principles it upholds, have an obligation to take care in picking the battles at which to fight back and claim First Amendment protection. In exercising this selective discernment, nothing is more important than to distinguish between using the amendment to protect the people's right to know and using it as a smokescreen for a news organization's wrongdoing. If news organizations do not make this distinction, regulatory bodies and authorities will be more than happy to step in and do the job. Often there is a powerful temptation for news organizations to try to argue a defense by crying "First Amendment" when they are attacked, especially in the courts. But it is hard for outside observers to be persuaded that the First Amendment, protector of individual conscience against institutional authority, was meant as a private guardian for the large, entrenched media organizations that are parties to these cases. Instead, the use of First Amendment arguments by the press looks like a disguise to hide less high-minded, more selfish motives.

Should I be pressed to summarize the ethical guidelines for the media into one principle I would say this: truth is to be the one guiding light in all endeavors. From this will stem all other desirable practices of a good newspaper or publisher: fairness, accuracy, honesty, responsibility and decency. I remember one instance that proved to me that truth is far from being the driving force for many publications. I was the CEO of an organization which operated, among other community outreach programs, a childcare center. One disgruntled parent had gone to the two leading newspapers in the area with a false report claiming that our childcare center was guilty of serious child abuse on a sustained basis. Both newspapers called the Center to verify the story. They were both informed that the story was baseless and that the Division of Children and Youth would be issuing a statement within a few hours once their investigation was completed. One of the newspapers, obviously with ethical management at the helm, waited for the report and printed the facts. The other newspaper, without any interest in the truth, printed the false story without waiting. They later were forced to print a retraction, but the harm had already been done and could not be easily rectified. From then on, this incident provoked me to look at any printed story with a more skeptical eye. How much of what we read or hear has been regurgitated without properly checking the facts first? I would like to think that the paper that printed the incorrect story would lose credibility. Hopefully, a loss of credibility would result in a decline in readership and this would cause them to look into their own organization with a critical eye and correct their unethical practices.

The advent of new technology brings fresh challenges such as those that accompany the booming spread of the Internet. It applies both to entertainment sites as well as to journalistic sites. New media create unique issues because of the new applications of technology which enable innovative practices. We now not only find advertisements on the same page as the articles, but they can also be embedded within the article itself in the form of a hyperlink. Either way, linking articles to commerce is far more immediate and effective online. Readers or viewers quickly become "consumers". While a print advertisement requires you to remember the ad and visit a store to make a purchase, all it takes online is a click of the mouse. Should a reputable newspaper on their online version include a link to a bookseller's website directly below a book review? Can the reviewer be expected to remain indifferent to the fact the their advertiser would sell many more copies of the book if the review is favorable, or conversely, that a poor review would hurt the bookseller's revenue?

In this world of noise and haste, the need for speed fosters the growth of tabloid press and television. The accelerated pace and immediacy of access to hundreds of sources of information and entertainment creates a feeding frenzy in the search for items that will attract our attention. There is no time to unveil the truth behind the façade, so we merely receive as much of the proprietors easily obtained material and prejudice as the advertisers won't object to. There is an endless supply of characters lurking on the sidelines for their chance at their fifteen minutes of fame: the quirky leader of a sect who claims to have cloned the first human baby but refuses to submit to scientific tests to prove it, the butler who betrays the trust of his deceased employer and reveals intimate and irrelevant details of her private life and correspondence, the voluptuous widow who marries a millionaire in his deathbed and promptly recovers from her bereavement to capitalize on her celebrity as the star of her very own reality-television show, and so many others that never cease to amaze us with their brash hunger for publicity. One of the types of programs that bemuses me, not in a very pleasant way I have to say, are the reality shows on television. It seems to me that a parade of situations showing misfortune or disaster or embarrassment invoke interest and even addiction from a wide audience. Yet the parade appears to be completely without empathy, completely without any sense of rapport. In some of these shows a group of people is selected to be placed in a situation where their wits are put to the test, either with gruesome or exhausting physical trials or by a strained cohabitation with strangers that brings out the worst aspects of their nature. If contestants would joyfully get along and relate to each other in a civilized way these shows would have zero ratings. The attraction is of course, the conflict, the human ferocity. Are we simply enjoying other people's misfortunes? Is television increasingly exploiting catastrophe in order to attain higher ratings? There are plenty of zones in television where the absence of ethics is precisely the source of fascination. It seems that what is offered is not art or information but just entertainment that is intended to be consumed like fast-food, and promptly forgotten in a rabid search for the next quick snack. It makes us wonder what kind of people we are. We can claim that children are innocent victims being manipulated by marketing tactics, but as adults we have complete choice and control over our viewing habits. We are not being involuntarily exposed to these shows or websites as we are to billboard advertising on the side of the road, which we can hardly avoid seeing. Hardly so. Whenever we watch these shows or look at these websites we become active accomplices in the exchange. As viewers or readers, we can select the material that we are interested in consuming. We are therefore, bound by the same ethical values as for every other choice in our lives. When we download music from a free web service, we are violating the artist's intellectual property rights. When we watch somebody else being humiliated on television we are participating in the humiliation. The mere fact that we remain anonymous does not take away from the reality that, without viewers, the show would not go on. Advertisers pay for space on these shows because they know that our "eyeballs" will be watching and the success of these shows causes producers to seek out more shows of the same caliber. It then follows that by choosing what we watch today, we are actually choosing what will be available for us to watch in the future. Increasingly, children and young adults play out in the real world what they see on television, giving the term "reality TV" a new self-fulfilling, frightening dimension.

In contrast, there are programs that show us how to cook, garden, and improve our home among other things. So these shows, while they appear to offer mere technical advice, also promote certain sorts of ethical values: cooking is good; do-it-yourself, building your own deck is good for you; recycling and composting in your garden is virtuous, using non-chemical sprays in your garden is ethically important. All these shows promote certain sorts of conducts over others, and in that they are making ethical suggestions and they are saying to the viewer, 'Think about yourself in ethical terms; think about yourself and your actions in terms of what's right, what's wrong, what's better, what's worse.' I am not suggesting that the only way to be a good person is to cook every meal from scratch and slave away in the garden all weekend; but rather that as a consumer of the media, it is up to you to choose what enriches and enlightens you and to discard what doesn't.

Journalists and editors everywhere have the vital role to provide the public with information, knowledge and understanding. But as they practice their craft in a world that is both technologically and geographically changing, systematic standards must guide their work. Only in that way will the media serve their society in an ethically responsible and constructive fashion. I do not believe in censorship or in a centralized entity to impose ethical standards on the media. Our constitution guarantees the freedom of the press and of expression, which ensures a press largely without governmental regulation. In any case, these standards would be virtually impossible to enforce and they would overlap with the existing judicial system that already deals with such issues as copyright infringement, plagiarism, libel and defamation. What the media needs is a self imposed high-code of ethics to both guide and monitor their operations. The best format for this body would be a committee at the local level, composed by representatives from the advertisers and the readership, to ensure that the community is not being ignored to favor the interests of the advertising revenue. These committees should never be perceived as a threat or encumbrance to the media. To the contrary, these committees should help the media align themselves with the values prevailing in the communities they cater to, and they would also serve to field complaints before they snowball into costly legal actions. The committee would have an ear close to the ground to be able to warn the media when they have crossed the line. A well-publicized code of ethics would send out a clear message to the audience as to the values upheld by the particular publication or broadcaster.

Bottom line, although the technology and the channels of information and entertainment have evolved, the rules haven't changed much. We must hope that credibility will continue to be a factor of success. We hope that the media will remember that they are not writing for consumers or investors, but for intelligent citizens, who have wide concerns and interests and who care deeply about the state of their community, their nation and the environment that their children will inherit. And we hope that we will all keep in mind the admonishment found in Mathew 12:36 - "But I say unto you, that every idle word that men shall speak, they shall give account thereof in the day of judgment."

14. Ethics and Civil Disobedience

When is Transgression of Social Laws Morally Permissible?

As indicated at the conclusion of the discussion addressing situational ethics, one of the longstanding debates among theologians has been the challenge of reconciling the moral authority of God with the legal control of the governing bodies that order society. Since the time of Christ, the conflict between religious beliefs and civil society has been a serious dilemma for Christians. In Christ's era, His evangelical activities were contrary to the prevailing laws and social norms, and the radical message of Christianity was ultimately punished by His crucifixion.

Today, Christians in Western societies are not subject to death as a result of their beliefs. In fact, the widespread prevalence of the Christian faith has established it as the major religion throughout much of the West. Although this predominance would seem to lend itself to facilitating Christian-friendly social policy, the trend towards secularism in recent decades has resulted in the development and implementation of many policies that the majority of Christians are uncomfortable with, with the most ubiquitous example being legalized abortion.

From an ethical standpoint, what are Christians to do when they feel that prevailing laws of society are in opposition to the chief principles of Christian morality? Throughout the New Testament, Jesus exhorts His followers to adhere to the civil laws governing society. At the same time, however, the ultimate dictate of Christian faith is maintaining unconditional loyalty to God's moral authority. When these two pillars of authority are in conflict, the consequences can be highly confusing for believers seeking to reconcile the two spheres of civil and divine rule. One of the most pressing ethical concerns for current-day Christians is achieving a point that successfully balances these two codes.

However, as alluded to previously, there are some instances in which Christians find the civil government's position on a particular matter to be wholly indefensible and inconsistent with any framework of Christian ethical decision-making. In these cases, some believers have found it necessary to engage in civil disobedience, which is typically defined as a form of non-violent protest.

Throughout the twentieth century, the practice of civil disobedience has come to be regarded as a noble, dignified form of highlighting social ills that has been put to use in advancing the admirable causes of peace and social equality by such luminaries as Mahatma Gandhi and Martin Luther King, Jr.

At the same time, it must be acknowledged that civil disobedience is, at root, a form of illegal activity that violates standing civil laws.

The ethical dilemma for Christians arises from determining when the moral offensiveness of a civil law merits civil disobedience. In recent years, this debate has generated a significant amount of controversy. During this period, many of the more fundamentalist Christian groups have increasingly distanced themselves from the government, seeming to flout the sovereignty and legal authority of civil society on an ever-widening array of issues. At the same time, Christian protestors decrying the practice of legalized abortion have resorted to increasingly violent measures in order to impede the continuation of this legal, but ethically questionable activity.

This discussion will address the question of civil disobedience within the larger framework of Christian ethics. Both sides in the civil disobedience debate will be considered and analyzed with references to past and current instances of laws that have been deemed immoral by believers. In conclusion, an overview of the ethicality of engaging in civil disobedience from a Christian standpoint will be presented.

The earliest documented case of Christian civil disobedience is the stance taken by early church members against the prevailing law that was intended to disallow Christian proselytizing. Throughout the book of Acts, the disciples' decision to flout the law and continue with their evangelical outreach is documented. For Christians, their action is clearly beneficial from a moral standpoint. However, they were in clear violation of stated civil laws, and in deciding to ignore these laws through sustained civil disobedience, the early church members put themselves seriously at risk.

There are a number of different camps within the debate about the moral and ethical permissibility of civil disobedience among Christians. Some argue that ethical Christians should not engage in civil disobedience, due to the many statements that Jesus made that assert the importance of obeying civil authorities. Others take the position that Christians should engage in civil disobedience to protest laws that are morally offensive in a Christian framework, but they are not morally obligated to do so. The most extreme position in the debate holds that Christians are ethically obligated by their beliefs to protest and disobey those laws that they view to be morally impermissible.

Some of the most visible supporters of the latter position are those Christians engaged in the pro-life, anti-abortion movement. For example, the leadership of the militant Operation Rescue group, which has been involved or suspected in a number of violent attacks at abortion clinics, endorses the view that Christians are obligated to take direct action against civil laws that are inherently opposed to the Christian ethical system.

Throughout the Old Testament and the New Testament, there are copious examples of individuals who make the brave decision to contravene existing, morally indefensible laws and who are subsequently looked upon favorably by God and/or Jesus as a direct result of their decision to engage in civil disobedience. One of the most frequently cited Old Testament accounts involves the story of Rahab, recounted in Joshua 2:1-14, in which a prostitute transgresses the existing law by concealing two of Joshua's Hebrew spies from the military forces seeking them.

In this account, Rahab's brave decision to engage in blatant civil disobedience gains God's favor and results in the safekeeping of her family amidst the wholesale destruction of their community, clearly as a result of having gained God's favor through her act of defiance against the existing civil authority. This is merely one of myriad examples in which God favors those who engage in civil disobedience against laws that are unjust or unfairly persecuting of certain classes of people (cf. Acts 4, Daniel 3, and Exodus 5).

The clearest statement on civil disobedience and when it is ethically permissible for Christians is given in Acts 5:28-29. In this passage, it is explicitly stated that Christians should only ignore the civil laws when they command citizens to commit acts that are overtly evil, or to disallow acts that are morally beneficial. However, as with the ambiguity surrounding the question of situationism versus absolutism in ethical decision-making, this passage can be interpreted in many different ways, as evidenced by the broad array of responses that current-day Christians have evidenced.

For example, militant pro-life groups have asserted that this passage and other similar biblical exhortations are tantamount to requiring active civil disobedience on the part of Christians. The other side of the debate, based on a more moderate interpretation of this scripture, holds that no civil disobedience need be undertaken unless the government is forcibly requiring unethical actions on the part of Christian individuals. For example, some countries in Asia had once implemented forced-abortion laws as a desperate measure to control population growth. From even the most moderate interpretation of scripture, such a law would require civil disobedience on the part of Christians. However, in actuality, it is rarely the case that the government mandates behavior that is unethical from a Christian stance, so from this perspective, civil disobedience would rarely be wholly justified.

While this explanation of the debate over the mandate upon Christians to engage in civil disobedience may lend the impression that the decision to disobey immoral laws should be a relatively simple process, it must be acknowledged that the problem of individual interpretation once again problematizes the decision-making process. The task of interpreting what comprises an "evil" act or the prevention of carrying out morally beneficial acts (which are the criteria set forth for civil disobedience in Acts 5:28-29, as discussed above) lies with the individual believer.

As such, any hope of objectively or uniformly applying these standards are overcome by the many variations in interpretation, personal agenda, and ideological leanings that tend to distinguish the different sects of Christians from one another. A law that one Christian may interpret as an inducement to commit evil may be regarded by another as simply another secular annoyance that can easily be overlooked. Once again, the problem of interpretation poses the greatest challenge to the development of a concise standard of ethical permissibility for civil disobedience for the Christian community.

While this debate seems to leave little room for Christians to work against legal or policy trends that they view as potentially deleterious without transgressing their own ethical obligations to respect civil authority, it must be pointed out that the active, willful decision to disobey an existing law is not the only option available for making one's opinion known.

One of the hallmarks of the United States and many other Western democracies is the right to engage in peaceful protests and demonstrations legally. As such, this legal option opens up many avenues for protest that do not involve the ethical transgression that may be involved when one decides to commit civil disobedience. Many politically active Christians are frequent protestors against policies that they view as morally suspect or potentially harmful, without taking the decisive step of themselves committing illegal acts in the course of protesting.

In addition, even among those Christians who do ultimately make the decision that they must engage in civil disobedience in order to protest a law that they see as inducing them to commit an evil act or refrain from doing good, there are multiple gradations of civil disobedience that can be undertaken. Today, among more radical camps of Christian activists, the term "civil disobedience" is often used as a euphemism for violent retaliation, but this is not an accurate characterization.

The civil disobedience campaigns led by Martin Luther King, Jr. against the segregation policies throughout the Southeast did not consist of violent actions. Instead, the protestors often engaged silently and stoically in legally forbidden acts such as sitting at a lunch counter designated as white only. Not only did these activists largely refrain from violent protest, much of the power of their symbolic gestures lay in their quiet dignity and refusal to stoop to the level of violence.

Even today, many of the Christian activists who protest against abortion rely on the type of civil disobedience techniques used by King and his followers, although the violent actions of fringe groups are often highlighted in media coverage. These examples reveal the insidious nature of the groups that claim that violent acts committed in the name of promoting an ethical Christian worldview can be justified as doctrinally-sanctioned civil disobedience.

While the New Testament is clear on the issue of civil disobedience, outlining some scenarios in which it is ethically justifiable for Christians to break existing civil laws, it is also similarly clear on assigning the prerogative of violence and/or military action to the civil authorities. Therefore, those Christians who engage in violence as a means of preventing immoral actions deemed legal under existing law are committing acts regarded as highly unethical according to Scripture.

At the same time, the Bible is clear on the point that Christians must disobey laws that induce us to commit immoral acts or disobey the Word of God. However, there are few existing laws that, when analyzed carefully, fully adhere to the standards set forth in Acts to necessitate civil disobedience. Once again, however, the problem of varying individual interpretations of concepts of moral behavior serves to render the determination of the ethicality of civil disobedience a highly complex process.

15. Ethics and Marriage

"God, the best maker of all marriages."
W. Shakespeare

The family is the social unit on which society comes into being and is perpetuated. We live in the wake of centuries of inherited social change, not only in economic, political and cultural institutions, but also in morals and ethical values. Yet as it was in centuries past, so it is today, the union of man and woman forms the essence of the family. It follows then that the strength and health of this union will reflect on the health and strength of society. Jesus exalted family relations and drew it as a primary symbol of God's relation to his people. He described this relationship as of Father and Son, and his own commitment to us as a marriage of Christ and Church. According to the teachings of Jesus, marriage is a Holy relationship, a bond not to be treated lightly. In marriage, the two parties are no longer two but one. The Church is one with Christ, as a husband is one with his wife. Marriage is an honorable estate, instituted by God, signifying a deep spiritual union. It is therefore to be entered advisedly and reverently.

It is worth noting that neither marriage nor abstention from marriage are in itself sacred, it is rather God's blessing upon either of these situations that sanctifies them. God's union of man and wife, male and female, is meant to be forever. Some of us choose a life of celibacy, others choose relationships that are not pleasing in God's eyes, such as cohabitation, promiscuous or same sex unions. And yet most adults choose to live in a marriage and family relationship. To these unions people bring their strengths and weaknesses, and as such it is not a simple relationship and it is very difficult to say what makes a "good" marriage. There are, however, three qualities that need to be present in every Christian marriage: love, faithfulness and respect. Let us look in more detail into these three elements.

It is important to distinguish between what I call "emotional love" and "spiritual love". No marriage is likely to be successful without strong ties of emotional love. This kind of love is based on deep emotion and desire. It is this attraction that brings people to know each other and consider sharing the rest of their lives together. While this is certainly a healthy and desirable element, it is unlikely that this emotional love alone will carry the couple over the multitude of irritations and obstacles that they are likely to encounter in a marriage. There is a second kind of love necessary, that I call "spiritual love" which suggests compatibility and common interests, and has deeper elements of friendship and affection. Emotional love is oriented towards self-gratification, spiritual love to selfless-giving. The presence of both types of love is a key ingredient to the success of the union.

Faithfulness is rooted to spiritual love and is a vital element of the Christian union. It is the glue that holds the marriage together through stormy days. Faithfulness will remain permanent, even when physical charms inevitably fade. Man has a biological and spiritual nature. As a biological creature it is subject to natural necessities. The sex impulse is a biological impulse designed to propagate the species, it is the instrument of ongoing life. Yet in the human sphere, sex has more to offer, in the higher expression of spiritual devotion, fidelity and love. In the same way, a family more than a temporal nest in which to procreate, is the nucleus in which the qualities of love and faithfulness are experienced and nurtured. It is therefore natural for us to experience physical appetites, but God requires of us rational and responsible action. Hedonistic self-gratification will lead to pain and suffering. In marriage man and wife become one so it is not possible for one half to hurt the other without hurting itself as well. Extramarital relations or even premarital relations do not carry the component of commitment that marriage embraces, there is no pledge of fidelity, and no assumption of permanent responsibilities. These relations are for self-gratification alone, and as such lack the spiritual grace of the married state. The sex relation between man and woman was instituted by God for marriage. The covenant of fidelity, when breached, strikes a mortal blow to the bond of marriage, but brings unending joy and comfort when it is upheld.

The third vital element of a healthy Christian marriage is respect. Within the marriage, and the family, each member will have the same importance. This does not mean that they will have the same function or duties, as these vary according to age, maturity and circumstance. It means that each person will enjoy the fullest dignity and opportunity for self-development and growth. No member of the marriage shall be exploited by the other, neither for self-gratification nor for gain. This respect means that each member of the family will regard the other as infinitely precious, such as God regards each one of us. In practical terms respect means giving each other space for solitude, practicing kindness, refraining from the use of angry words, and accommodate for differences in tastes and personality. In summary, to fulfill the promise of the marriage vows to love, comfort and honor the other. The sexual relation between husband and wife also requires the same level of respect, as a physical manifestation of the spiritual love for each other.

Any marriage that combines love, fidelity and respect has a high chance of success. The first stage of emotional love will most likely develop into a higher level of devotion, leading husband and wife together into a state of grace. It is in the midst of this love that the most fertile environment for bringing up children is found. Children raised in such a home will develop a sense of trust that will allow them to reach out into the world with initiative and independence. This family climate cultivates in the child personal characteristics such as responsibility, resilience and resourcefulness, traits that will carry the child boldly into adulthood.

Having made this broad brush stroke of the shape and form of the Christian marriage, it is necessary to acknowledge the alarming number of marriages that do not conform to this ideal, which brings us to the painful matter of divorce. When two people become one, it is not possible to divide them again into two neat halves. The two partners to a marriage have grown inextricably linked to each other through infinite sinewy ties. In a separation there is no clean cut, but a searingly painful rupture. Is it therefore legitimate to dissolve a marriage? Divorce is a breach of the true intent of marriage. Jesus condemns divorce, except for unchastity (Mathew 5:32 and 19:9). Adultery appears to be the only justification for divorce in the Bible. In our time, we may find that there are times when it is better for the marriage to end if it is destroying one of the partners for whatever reason. Divorced persons can certainly remarry without the stain of sin, but not until they have satisfied their relationship with the Lord and have sought and received good counseling. It is therefore easier to define what divorce is not intended for. Divorce is not intended to be the answer to a selfish personal indulgence. It is not justified when one simply tires of a mate and desires to marry another. It is not justified in selfish disregard of the effect of such a broken home upon the children and extended family and friends. People today are exposed to an individualistic culture that claims that if divorce is better for the adults, then it will be better for the children too. The focus of a marital kinship in terms of an ethical obligation to another has turned into an obligation to the self. Parents do not subordinate their interest to their children's, instead, individual happiness seems to be the standard by which a marriage is measured. However, it is not possible to pretend that divorce is an individual choice without a profound social effect. The truth is that while divorce may relieve some of the burden of obligation from the adults, it unloads the hardship on the children. It has been said that it is not healthy to stay in a marriage for the sake of the children. I disagree. This view presents marriage as merely an institution for the self-fulfillment of adults. Children have an ethical priority. Adults are more resilient than children and can be expected to sacrifice some of their own interests in order to preserve the stability necessary for their children to flourish. Children in divorced families are cheated out of their opportunity to grow into healthy, balanced adults. Studies have shown that these children are more likely to develop emotional and behavioral problems such as delinquency, school drop-out and drug use. The disruption of the family unit erodes the children's sense of identity and ability to commit themselves and sustain a long-term relationship. This is too high of a price to pay for marital dissatisfaction or boredom, or the appearance of another romantic interest. The easy and speedy divorces widely available today seriously damage the network of our society and endanger the very foundation of the family.

Indeed, the spiritual path is far from straight. We get ourselves twisted into spiritual traps that are very difficult to overcome. We are all sinners and we are bound to make mistakes and hurt others, even without any bad intentions. Sin is forgivable, and the Bible places no limit in the number of times that one can be forgiven. This does not mean, however, that sin, even when forgiven, will not carry heartbreaking consequences. In a marriage, there are a multitude of evils that can wedge a fracture in the intimacy of the relationship. The list is virtually limitless. All that is needed to grow the most pernicious weeds is a small crack in the foundation. If you are going to succeed and maintain an intimate long-term marriage, you must take the matter very seriously. The natural course of things will tend to push you away from one another, not bring you together. Harmony is an everyday job. Some of the evils that trip up a relationship are very evident, and others creep up slowly, almost unnoticed until they have become major obstacles. Among the most common factors that threaten marriages are:

- Conflicts over how the money should be handled
- Infidelity
- Exhausted partners overwhelmed by the demands of careers, child-raising, and housekeeping
- Interference from in-laws
- Substance abuse, gambling, and other addictions
- Verbal or physical abuse

Premarital counseling is a must and can literally save a marriage. The bride and groom often enter into marriage with an array of their own assumptions and unrealistic expectations about life after the wedding. That is because a dating relationship is designed to conceal information, not reveal it. Each partner presents his or her best side, hiding embarrassing facts, habits, flaws, and personality traits. Then major conflict occurs a few weeks later when they discover they have radically different views on substantial issues. The stage is then set for arguments and hurt feelings that were never anticipated during the courtship period. How will you beat the odds? How will you build a solid relationship that will last a lifetime? How will you include yourselves among that seemingly endangered species of older couples who have garnered decades of happy memories and experiences? Even after forty or fifty years, they still look to one another for encouragement and understanding. They speak to each other with caring and affection. Their children have grown up in a stable and loving environment and have no ugly scars or bitter memories to erase. Only love prevails. That is the way God intended it to be, and it is still possible to achieve. Only with determination and hard work will you be able to preserve the love with which you began, but it is true that when you reach this level of mutual affection and understanding, there is very little in life that can provide such heartwarming joy.

Premarital counseling also helps identify areas of concern such as hesitancy to express feelings, or the possibility that the couple may be rushing into marriage too quickly due to pressure or fear. It also helps determine if a partner has poor listening skills and encourage awareness and couple discussion of strengths and weaknesses, readiness for marriage, and goals that should be met before marrying. Counseling is not intended to be like a crystal ball that predicts marital happiness. Rather, the results are used as a way to focus discussions between partners on developing strengths and overcoming weaknesses before they marry. This is important to do because weaknesses that exist before marriage and are unknown or ignored usually develop into bigger problems after marriage. Additionally, since couples in the premarital stage of their relationship are usually younger, happier, and more emotionally engaged and more highly committed to their relationship than at any other time in their lives, it makes sense to have these discussions before marriage. Counseling increases the chances of success for the couple in setting goals for improvement, and discussing other important topics related to marriage such as finances, roles in marriage, and having children. Premarital counseling also helps the couple improve their communication skills. Most couples rate premarital counseling as very helpful, and it also establishes in their relationship a positive attitude about seeking help if marriage problems arise in the future. In this respect, Christian couples have already an advantage in their favor by sharing the same belief and values.

God intended marriage to be a sacred, forever union between man and wife. Don't permit the possibility of divorce to enter your thinking. Even in moments of great conflict and discouragement, divorce is no solution. It merely substitutes a new set of pains for the ones you left behind. Guard your relationship against erosion as though you were defending your very lives. Invite God into your home and into your daily married life. Yes, you can make it together.

Not only can you survive, but you can keep your love alive if you give it priority in your system of ethical values.

16. Ethics and Parenting

"Train a child in the way he should go,
and when he is old he will not turn from it."
Proverbs 22:6

Nature or Nurture? The question of whether the root of behavioral and social problems in children and teenagers can be traced back to their parents or rather to the circumstances surrounding their upbringing is one that has long occupied the psychological profession. There are solid arguments on both sides, and parents attempting to make light of the different academic theories may find themselves confused. But there is one thing that all parents should know: even if it turns out that the genes they pass on and the friends their children play with have a significant role in influencing their child, parents have the power to open doors.

Parents are the primary providers of children while they are still in the household. They provide food, shelter and clothing. This is just but half the child's needs. It is not so much what we do for our children but what we teach them to do for themselves that will make them successful human beings. Affection, discipline and good example are the elements required to provide well-rounded parental nourishment.

Being a parent is a duty. To some of us, parenthood arrives by choice, as in the case of planned families or adoptive parents. To others, it arrives by "accident" as a result of unsafe sex. Whichever way it comes, parenthood is perhaps the bravest challenge we will ever undertake. It is a hard job - a dirty job. Quite often raising children is a thankless job. But nothing parents do for their children is ever wasted. Children may seem not to notice, remain indifferent, and seldom offer any thanks or appreciation, but what we do for our children is never wasted. The training that the child receives in the home will be the foundation they will lean on when it comes time to face future challenges.

Parents have the primary responsibility of presenting a value system to their children. In order to do this, they first need to be confident that they know what their own values are. This means much more than words. It may be tempting to assume that the act of dictating a desired behavior to a child is all that is needed. The real challenge, however, lies in the fact that the child will probably not listen attentively to what we say, but will notice every detail of what we do. If the two are inconsistent, the message will be lost. If we try to impress on a teenager the importance of driving responsibly while we are holding the steering wheel with one hand and a beer in the other, it is unlikely that the lesson will be taken seriously. If however, this same teenager has observed both parents - back from the days in the booster seat - always driving carefully, making sure their seatbelts are buckled, following the designated driver system when going to a party to make sure that whoever is driving hasn't consumed alcohol, it is likely that although he or she may still choose to drive recklessly, this teenager will at the very least be well aware of the high risk involved in such behavior.

In order to communicate to your children a sense of personal conscience you need to establish and sustain a dialogue. A meaningful exchange of perceptions needs to be conducted, in order to be effective, in a climate of support, safety and understanding. Dialogue does not involve words alone. Sometimes you can communicate more with a nod or even a well-timed silence. Usually when we interact with other adults, as with our peers at work or at a social occasion, we respond to their posture or attitude, we may say "You seem a little down, is everything OK?" We need to do the same with our children. We need to ask open questions. Instead of asking "Did you have a good day?" that can receive a yes or no for an answer, we can ask, for example: "What happened today?" As children grow up, they attempt to establish their own identity and sometimes refuse to participate or present resistance to any attempt at dialogue. It is important to tune in to body language and allow for differences in dialogue styles. Some children are rather quiet, others talk a lot. Some children are simply slower to respond. It is also important to establish a non-judgmental tone in the conversation. If there is any objectionable action that needs to be discussed, it needs to be made clear that the issue is about the particular behavior and that we are not making any judgments about the person (the child). Once we establish a ritual of dialogue in the household, young people will come naturally out of their shell and participate.

Children will not duplicate exactly their parent attitudes, they will develop their own. Instilling discipline and values does not guarantee results. It is not unusual to wonder how a young person went astray with such dedicated parents, or to be amazed to see one sibling in a family thrive while another seems to always be embroiled in endless troubles. We hear the perennial argument between strictness and permissiveness. In my view, neither one will do the trick. Strictness is excessive manipulation or control by adults. It causes those controlled to feel powerless and frustrated. Children who do not perceive that they have power over their environment will often seek power in destructive ways. Strictness gives young people the option to either give in or rebel. Permissiveness on the other hand, produces insecurity and the impression that there is very little cause and effect in life. Permissiveness trains young people to manipulate other people into their service. The desirable point is in the middle of the two extremes. The optimal discipline is dispensed in an environment in which children can safely learn to exert their own power and it is achieved trough gentle, firm and consistent setting of reasonable limits within the context of family life. The objective is to develop discipline that works from inside the child rather than imposed by an authoritarian figure. Authoritarian discipline is faster, and may sometimes be necessary, as in the case where the child is about to cross the street without looking or touch a scalding surface. This is hardly the time to engage in a democratic debate about the proper course of action. The weakness of the authoritarian method is that whenever the authority figure is not present, the behavior will not be followed. The democratic approach involves the child in determining the proper codes of behavior and delineating the limits. When the child is trusted with increasing responsibilities and is allowed to learn by experience, it develops self-discipline. This system provides a navigation guide that children will later be able to use in making decisions as adults. Out of this environment children will develop self-trust, pride, initiative and resourcefulness. They will also be more apt at functioning in groups in their adult life, whether in a family, job or community environment. Laissez faire, or no leadership at all, leads to chaos. The conscience of children is formed by the influences that surround them, their notions of good and evil are the result of the moral atmosphere they breathe. Children that are not exposed to this navigation system in their early years may never have the opportunity to develop it. These will indeed be deprived children, no matter how affluent their environment may be in every other respect.

I remember when I was engaged to the young lady who became my wife forty-eight years ago. We were enrolled in a premarital counseling course at the University of Kansas City. The professor, during one of the counseling sessions, stated that there is no way to buy disasterproof insurance for your children to guarantee that they will not watch too much TV or be too influenced by the wrong crowd, or become involved with drugs or addicted to alcohol or end up in a destructive relationship that is doomed to fail. The best way to insulate a child form the corruption that is rampant in our society is for the parents to instill in their children the highest ethical values based upon the teaching of the Lord and through His Word. In order to accomplish this essential task, parents need to teach by example and not wait for someone else to turn up as a role model. Parents need to spend time with their children, both talking and listening. Most importantly, parents need to bring their children into the presence of the Lord. The young boy and girl trained in the teachings of the Bible will have a moral reliance which will serve as a compass for everyday living. They will know the difference between right and wrong, good and evil. They will be able to conquer the temptations of life.

Discipline serves to correct the baseness of human passions, it fortifies the heart and mind with virtuous principles, and furnishes enjoyment from within. It is of more consequence to general happiness than all the provisions of goods and fortune. Of all the lessons you teach your child, if only two lessons were to remain, then all your efforts have been a triumph. The two guiding Christian principles: to love God and to love your brethren. These should be at the root of any discipline or lesson imparted to our children. The aim is to instill these lessons in your child so that he or she will be dependable even if they are not being watched (especially when they are not being watched). From these stem all the characteristics you would desire your children to possess: Courtesy, kindness, sincerity, truthfulness, thoughtfulness and good manners.

All children come to this world with the capacity for idealism, creativity and spirituality. The future depends on them. Generation after generation have failed embarrassingly to solve enormous, frightening problems in our world. Yet they have also achieved phenomenal accomplishments in science, technology, knowledge, arts and sports. But as our material lives grew richer, our spiritual lives have become the poorer. We would do well to bring up our children with a feeling that they are in this world not only for their own satisfaction but essentially to love and serve others. Children are proud to think that they can be truly useful and will rise to the challenge. Even very young children should not be allowed to think that they can deliberately break something or make a mess but that they owe respect. Parents should expect something from their children. I don't mean a formal thank-you note for being born or cared for; but parents have reason to expect consideration, affection, and willingness to accept the family's standards and limits. If parents are too hesitant to ask for reasonable behavior, either because they are afraid their children will dislike them or because they are self-sacrificing in nature, they may grow to resent the bad behavior and become angry. Parents can't feel affectionate towards their children if they are bitter and angry underneath, and children will perceive these feelings and feel unhappy. Therefore, in order to have happy children you need to make them behave. And since parents are only human, and patience is not unlimited, there will be times when you will feel anger. When a child disobeys a well understood and reasonable rule, it is hard for parents to remain cool. Some parents are in touch with these feelings and even joke about it. When you ask them "How is the baby?" they'll laugh and reply "Adorable...would you like to keep him for a few months?" Being able to recognize that they are losing their temper helps them control their anger and blow it off faster. Some parents set impossible standards for themselves, and feel that good parents should never feel angry. These repressed feelings will only make them tired and tense, and this tension will be felt by the children. It isn't shameful to admit being irritated as a fact of life, and the sooner we do it the sooner we can clear the air. Increasingly children are bombarded with anger and aggression in the media, and the way these matters are dealt with in the home will help them deal with the world beyond their doorstep.

Children are exposed to brutality in television, movies, books, the Internet. It is relatively easy to control the influence of the media with very young children, but as they grow older and more independent, the means to shield them from this influence grow weaker. The same goes for influence exerted by their peers, friends at school or in the playground. If you think of how many hours in the day a child is exposed to all these influences, it makes you realize all the more how very precious are the few hours of meaningful interaction in the home. Every opportunity should be taken to engage in dialogue and share quality time together. Television time should be limited. In family conversations children should hear about the problems of their communities or current events happening in the world around them. It is important for parents not to focus on developing intellect alone. Parents may feel pressured to make sure that their child grows up "smart" and therefore stimulate learning by intellectual means alone. Mental capacity is only one aspect of a person. Well-rounded development depends on a foundation of feelings of love and trust. Children reach out to their parents and other adults and build relationships based on the response they receive. A child that receives warm smiles and hugs, and food when he is hungry and comfort when he is in pain will be able to better deal with ideas, concepts and interaction with others. The same goes for overemphasizing other aspects of the child's development, such as their physical beauty or athletic prowess. Children need to be appreciated for their whole personality, not primarily for their brains or looks or particular ability. It is good to appreciate a child's special gift, as long as it is considered a part of the whole person that they are.

It is my wish that every child that is born into this world arrives because he is wanted, and has the opportunity to grow up and become a happy and productive member of society. It is my wish for parents that they be able to rejoice in their children, as an aged man reclining under the shadow of a beautiful tree which he has himself planted.

17. Ethics and Abortion

"Children are a heritage of the Lord;
and the fruit of the womb a reward from him."
Psalms 127:3

People seem to be irretrievably divided on the morality of abortion. There is a marked duality, as often reported in the media, that breaks camp into two distinct sides. Either you are pro-life, or you are pro-choice. The complexity increases because neither side is in full agreement over when, if ever, is a woman to have access to abortion.

The pro-life advocates, in general terms, argue that a human being becomes such at the very moment of conception. At this instant, a unique DNA is imprinted on the human being, and many believe it is at this time that God bestows a human soul in this single fertilized cell. Based on this belief, the voluntary termination of the embryo at any stage of the developing process is peremptorily termed as a form of homicide, and therefore considered immoral. There are varying degrees of absolutism in the pro-life position. There are some who claim that abortion should be outlawed under all conditions. To others, abortion is to be tolerated only when the continuation of the pregnancy would endanger the life of the mother. Many are prepared to accept abortion in extreme cases where conception is the result of rape or incest.

The pro-choice faction, in contrast, argues that a woman should have full control over her own body. Again, there are variations within this group. Some claim that a woman has the right to have a safe abortion at any time during the pregnancy, from conception all the way up to the moment of imminent birth. For others, the limit is the existence of life in the fetus which can be defined in opposition to the concept of death. Generally defined, death occurs when the brain ceases to have detectable activity, even though the heart and respiratory systems may still be functioning. Consequently the fetus is considered to be alive when it develops neurological activity which has been found to occur sometime around the fifth month with the development of the cerebral cortex. Others further argue that a woman has the right to terminate the pregnancy only up to the point where the fetus is viable. The fetus is considered viable at that stage of development when the baby is potentially able to live outside the mother's womb, even with artificial help. As a result of the advances in science and technology, there has been a vast increase in the effectiveness and complexity of the life support systems for premature babies. In the old days, it was believed that the baby was not alive until it started kicking in the mother's womb. As medical knowledge in this field advanced, babies were known to survive if born after their 30th week from conception. In our time, with the benefit of ultrasound imaging we are able to see with our eyes the miracle of life taking place from the very beginning. Babies have been known to survive outside the womb as early as their 21st week of gestation. Some day science will develop artificial methods for preterm infants to survive even earlier. We cannot assert with absolute conviction where the frontiers of viability lie.

A landmark day in the legality of abortion in our country was January 22, 1973. It was on this day that the Supreme Court decision was handed down in the case of Roe v. Wade. In the ruling of this controversial case the court declared that the abortion statutes of the State of Texas, which proscribed abortion except on medical advice to save the mother's life, were void. They found the statutes to be vague and overbroadly infringing a woman's right to privacy, her Ninth and Fourteenth Amendment rights. In the ruling, the justices acknowledge "the sensitive and emotional nature of the abortion controversy, of the vigorous opposing views, even among physicians, and of the deep and seemingly absolute convictions that the subject inspires. One's philosophy, one's experiences, one's exposure to the raw edges of human existence, one's religious training, one's attitudes toward life and family and their values, and the moral standards one establishes and seeks to observe, are all likely to influence and to color one's thinking and conclusions about abortion. In addition, population growth, pollution, poverty, and racial overtones tend to complicate and not to simplify the problem. "The task of the court, the ruling continues, is of course to resolve the issue by constitutional measurement, free of emotion and of predilection. But it is not our interest to discuss the dynamics of abortion in the court of law. Not so, for that matter, are we concerned with the courts of public opinion. Our sole focus in this discussion is to follow the teachings of Jesus.

The Bible does not provide us with a clear directive referring to abortion as such. In fact, in order to find our guidance, we have first to embrace the teachings of Jesus in their entirety. If we attempt to look at the Bible as an oracle, to find the specific verse to answer our question, we will fail to learn the lesson. We are in fact deluding ourselves into only finding the answers that we want to hear. In Luke 1:15 we learn that Jesus "shall be filled with the Holy Ghost, even from his mother's womb". Some translations reflect this to happen "from his birth". It apparently refers only to Jesus birth, but it is an acknowledgement of an unborn baby as having a soul. This is further affirmed in Luke 1:42 referring to the child that Mary is carrying: "blessed art thou amongst women, and blessed is the fruit of thy womb". Once again, this may interpreted to refer either only to Jesus, or to all babies even before they are born. We do know, at the very least, that the Bible refers with reverence to this pregnancy, both as regards the fetus as to the woman who is carrying it. Children are a gift from the Lord, to be preciously protected. To eliminate a human life is a sin. No matter how much we toss an argument around, there is no right way to do a wrong thing. As with all sin this, too, is forgivable. The love of God for us knows no boundaries or conditions, only those we impose ourselves in our human frailty. The fact that our sins can be forgiven does not mean that we can undo what has been done. It is our fate to live with the consequences and effects of our decisions, both physical and psychological, every single day thereafter. As Christians, we are called to abhor the sin of abortion, yet love and show compassion for all people. It is not our place to judge either the pregnant mother, or the physician who performs the procedure. Any form of violence, whether in the name of pro-choice or pro-life, goes against our Christian teachings. In the place of bombings, shootings, or unkind words let us offer the love of Christ.

It is tempting to imagine how we wish things to be, but we shouldn't lose sight of the way things really are. Over one million abortions take place each year. One out of six women in this country have resorted to the procedure. With numbers like these, odds are that if you haven't had an abortion yourself, you know someone who has. As Christians we have the power to bring about change. If you listen carefully to the testimony of women who have gone through an abortion, so many times you hear that they were not told about the procedure or the risks involved beforehand. If there is to be a choice, let it be an informed one. Women have a right to know what they are choosing. As a community, we should also make information available to these women on every possible alternative course of action. Women faced with the reality of an unwanted pregnancy are afraid and lonely. There are many reasons why abortion may seem to be the only road available. They either have financial concerns about their ability to raise a child, or they feel that the time is inconvenient because of their age, careers, or the fact that they are not married. Another factor is their fear of how others will judge them. In their despair they reason that if they can make the pregnancy disappear, no one will ever know. It is much later that they experience the mental anguish nobody ever told them about. Sadness, grief, guilt, loss. Sometimes they accept the Lord's forgiveness, but they find it harder to forgive themselves. Added to this mental and spiritual pain, they can also be experiencing physical residual effects related to the procedure. Are we doing everything we can for these women? If we could only embrace them while they are confronting their agonizing choice, show them that there are alternatives. If we could only help them find a way to obtain financial aid, somewhere to live, offer them our prayers, what difference our stewardship could make. If the parents of a young woman would express their unconditional love and respect for the women's decision. If the father of the baby would own up to his share of the bargain and lend emotional support and financial help, how many more babies would have a chance to live? We need to do more. We need to inform women of the possibilities of adoption. So many childless couples are eager and willing to provide a stable, loving home for those babies. It seems that we have two unmet needs, the biological mother confronted with the unwanted pregnancy, and the hopeful adoptive family confronted with their inability to procreate. It is not a perfect solution, but so seldom any solutions ever is. If we could alleviate one pain, and provide an opportunity for a baby to come to full term and have a chance at a prosperous life, wouldn't that be worth a try? Whenever we encounter a single mother, instead of jumping to judgment, we could perhaps find in our hearts the love to support and encourage her. She chose to face the challenge and keep her baby. Maybe we could even offer her our help, what a provoking thought. Maybe her friends and neighbors could offer babysitting services to give her some private time, or to run errands for her to ease the burden of her chores. Any small gesture, not the least of which would be to pray for her and her baby, would make a difference. Even if she never accepts the offer, she will know that a support system is there should she ever need it.

With the movement seeking equal rights for women along came many wonderful benefits, ranging from the ballot to the choice of a career outside the home. Unfortunately, an unwanted side effect was of the liberation was the equation of freedom with sexual promiscuity. Yet after years of "having it all" the feeling of emptiness remains. Education is the key to this labyrinth. By the time our sons and daughters arrive into adulthood they may be faced with the hard reality of an unwanted pregnancy. At that point we are powerless to do much except offer them alternatives such as adoption or support in raising the baby. Our work needs to be done at a much earlier stage, starting with sex education from the time children are old enough to ask questions. This information will help them develop their own values and ethics on the holiness of human life, and hopefully they will also have self-respect for their bodies and spiritual integrity and chose to wait to have sex until they marry. Sexual education seeks to reduce the risks of potentially negative outcomes such as unwanted pregnancies, sexually transmitted diseases or falling victims to abuse or exploitation. It also serves to develop young people's ability to make decisions over their entire lifetime, and to enhance the quality of their relationships. Young people often witness a wide range of attitudes and beliefs in relation to sexuality. This can sometimes be confusing. For example the messages they receive at home and at school may emphasize the risks and dangers associated with sexual activity, encouraging abstinence. In contrast, the media portrays young people who engage in sexual relations as seemingly more attractive or mature. I have found young people to be very interested in the moral and cultural framework surrounding sexuality. They often welcome the opportunity to discuss issues, such as abortion, even though they may giggle and act silly. Even when we think that it is important for our sons and daughters to abstain from sex until marriage, we need to be aware that they will ultimately make their own decisions, and we should not withhold information about safe sex and contraception. In fact, an open discussion will help young people reflect on the reason why they may want to have sex, and how it may affect their ethics and self-respect. It is evident that unless we keep an open line of communication, and sometimes even if we do, they will seek out this information in magazines, television, websites or from their peers. Some of this information will be helpful and accurate. Some will not. Sex education can be viewed as an ongoing conversation carried on over the years, mainly about ethical values while at the same time providing some facts. It is a conversation, not a lecture, since it is just as important to listen attentively as it is to impart information. The conversation will evolve as the young person grows more mature and is able to process more complex information. This conversation can be left off and picked up again at any opportunity, such as discussing something shown on television, or an item in the news. This conversation will take place over a range of situations and in different settings. For parents who are not sure about how to tackle this subject with their children, or wonder at what age to start, schools and teachers can provide guidance and sources of information to find the answers.

Babies are meant to arrive in this world surrounded by love. Children build the strength of a family and become the crown on their parent's lives. A baby is a symbol of growth, joy, delight. As Christians, let us do our share towards building a society where every baby is conceived in warm and loving anticipation; and where the news of a pregnancy is always cause for celebration.

18. Ethics and Cultural Diversity

The Ethical Imperative to Eradicate Racism

From the earliest days of the Christian church, the faith has been one that actively seeks to forge connections among groups that have historically been estranged from one another, to include those groups and individuals who have traditionally been marginalized and excluded, and to create love, unity, and solidarity where enmity and rancor have long existed. Particularly since the time of Christ's ministry, these objectives have been foregrounded as some of the chief aims of the faith.

Unfortunately, these aims have often been drastically misinterpreted or overlooked throughout the ensuing millennia, as historical, economic, social, and political forces often overcame the strength and influence of the Christian faith. In some instances, such as the institutionalized slavery that long existed in the United States, Christian doctrine and Scripture were often perverted as a means of justifying practices that served to elevate or privilege one group, class, or race of people over another.

Some of the most significant changes that transpired throughout the twentieth century involved the dismantling of many of the institutions and practices that supported racial discrimination and inequality. Today, racial and ethnic minorities enjoy a greater representation among the general population, as well as more political, social, and economic influence, than at any other time in American history. Indeed, according to recent Census data, it seems that the time is fast approaching in which the term "minority" will no longer be quite as applicable to describe groups co-existing within an increasingly diverse American population.

However, while many of the outward signs of racial discrimination have been dismantled, the actual social and cultural integration of the various racial and ethnic groups has not been equally successful. In some instances, the chasms separating these groups socially, economically, and politically have grown even more pronounced in recent years.

Certainly, the practice of Christianity has grown increasingly fractured along racial and ethnic lines throughout American communities; with a few exceptions, there are few Christian congregations that can rightfully be described as integrated. In spite of the fact that Jesus professed unconditional love of one's neighbors as one of the most important pillars of the Christian faith, our places of worship remain woefully segregated by race, ethnicity, and class.

Despite the increasing factionalization and compartmentalization of the Christian faith in the United States, one objective that virtually all Christian leaders agree upon is the ethical imperative to forge a religion that is united by faith of all races and ethnicities, rather than divided by these outward distinctions that Jesus repeatedly reminded us were superficial and largely meaningless from an ethical point of view. With the notable exception of the racial separatists that occupy the extreme right of the ideological spectrum, the need to effect a sense of healing reconciliation and integration is a goal shared by many leaders of the Christian church today.

However, at the current juncture, this type of sweeping racial and ethnic reconciliation carried out under the rubric of Christian fellowship has remained elusive. In the service of promoting an open dialogue on this topic, the current discussion will frame the issue of cultural diversity within the larger context of Christian ethics.

The primary topic that will be addressed will include the ethical imperative to cultivate racial and ethnic reconciliation among Christian believers. It will be argued that the achievement of a greater level of integration and reconciliation is necessary to ensure the continued vitality and relevance of Christianity within the rapidly changing social environment.

Because the issue of race and racism has increasingly entered the public discourse in recent years, the vocabulary of these debates has become familiar to most citizens who maintain even a moderate level of civic participation and political awareness. However, the issue of racial integration and reconciliation is very rarely figured within the context of religion, and even less frequently is the problem discussed within a Christian ethics framework. However, it is the position of many progressive church leaders that this perspective is sorely needed within the debate in order to effect the needed changes within the Christian community.

First and foremost, Christ's most frequent exhortation to His followers was the need to love one's neighbor as oneself. Despite the primacy of this dictate within the Christian religion, our flocks are still deeply and profoundly segregated by racial, ethnic, and class groups. It is the clear and indisputable duty of all Christians to work to eradicate the vestiges of racial discrimination and hatred, both within the larger culture and within themselves.

The only morally and ethically correct step to take in order to achieve this goal is to actively work to erase boundaries by overcoming racial divisions in churches and community groups. On an institutional level, Christian congregations must specifically seek to reach out to groups and individuals from divergent racial, ethnic, and class backgrounds.

However, it is also morally and ethically indefensible for Christians to rely on institutions to effect reconciliation between racial and ethnic groups. Just as sincere outreach efforts must be carried out at the institutional level, individual believers must also take it upon themselves to transcend racial and ethnic boundaries. Even seemingly insignificant gestures, such as engaging people of divergent backgrounds in casual conversation or making an effort to involve them in social gatherings or group outings, can have a positive cumulative effect in the long-term.

At the same time that all Christians must act upon their ethical duty to enact racial reconciliation, we must all accept the responsibility of doing so in a manner that is reflective and sensitive. Caucasian believers should carefully scrutinize the approach that they take in interacting with racially different people, in order to ensure that equality is the goal, rather than patronization or condescension. Most importantly, Christians from all backgrounds must accept personal responsibility to proactively engage with and forge connections with people from a wide variety of racial, ethnic, and class backgrounds.

While the ethical imperative for Christians to take the exhortation to love one's neighbor as oneself and apply it to the pressing problem of racial separation is simple, this is not to suggest that the process of achieving greater equality and reconciliation within the Christian community, as well as the larger culture, will be an easy task. The lingering uncertainty that many minorities harbor towards the dominant culture is completely understandable, given the centuries of oppression that many minorities have withstood in the United States.

Conversely, racial and ethnic minorities should be understanding of the potential for awkwardness and inaptitude that may characterize early outreach efforts in the process moving towards greater reconciliation. The presence of distinct cultural milieus that have come to largely exclude whites has eroded the ability of people from different racial, ethnic, and class backgrounds to easily find a common touchstone upon which to initiate communication. It must be expected that early phases of an outreach effort, no matter how well intentioned, will likely be difficult for all parties.

The issues of racial separation and inequality in Christian churches and among individual believers have been addressed, but another important issue must also be considered when discussing racial reconciliation from the standpoint of promoting Christian ethics. As discussed in the lesson on the ethics of civil disobedience, it was stated that Christians have an ethical obligation to disobey and protest laws that induce them to act immorally.

The chief dictum of Christian doctrine is to love one's neighbor as oneself, and for this reason many theologians see this as a call to consciously and deliberately transcend racial, ethnic, and class barriers in the attempt to promote Christian fellowship. As such, it also follows that Christians have an ethical obligation to protest any laws, policies, organizations, or institutional structures that tend to foment racial inequality.

Because legal, overt race-based discrimination has long been forbidden in the United States, we are sometimes lulled into a sense of complacency regarding the continued existence of institutionalized racism and racial discrimination. Sadly, these phenomena remain pervasive throughout twenty-first century American culture. Even today, the vestiges of institutional racism linger on, as evidenced most clearly by the socioeconomic disadvantage that continues to plague many racial and ethnic minority groups.

Throughout both the Old Testament and the New Testament, the scripture is replete with passages that demonstrate the disfavor that God holds towards social inequality, persecution, and oppression. Myriad verses instruct believers to undertake whatever action is necessary in order to achieve social justice in God's name. Jesus, in particular, frequently reiterated the need to deliberately seek out and offer succor to those who have been overlooked, marginalized, or oppressed by society. In many of His interactions with groups of people, Christ frequently made a point of emphasizing the need to help those deemed worthless by society.

Indeed, it is often overlooked that the Bible as a whole is highly concerned with identifying and reforming the corrupt social structures that tend to promote oppression, inequality, and persecution. Both Old Testament and New Testament verses reveal the primary importance of this objective within a framework of Christian ethics. It is frequently pointed out that if a Christian lives under an ethically sound government, there will be no conflict between serving God and adhering to the laws put forth by the civil authorities. However, when government institutions are corrupt and discriminatory, the potential for a conflict between these two realms increases precipitously.

Taken together, it is apparent that the dictates of Jesus on the subject of helping the marginalized, disenfranchised, and oppressed extend an ethical imperative for Christians to make every effort to eliminate discriminatory, inequitable policies at the institutional level in order to fulfill the command to love one's neighbor as oneself. If a "neighbor" of another race, ethnicity, or class is being discriminated against by a government organization or institution, and a Christian from the white cultural majority does not stand up against these practices, the dictate of loving one's neighbor as oneself is necessarily being undermined.

Without pandering excessively to the misguided efforts of the political correctness movement, who typically figure whites as the culpable enemy and racial minorities as wholly blameless in their plight, Christians from the dominant cultural majority do have an ethical obligation to acknowledge their own complicity in the oppression of racial and ethnic groups. Because the history of the United States is literally sodden with the blood of racial and ethnic minorities who were sacrificed at the altar of our country's economic supremacy, every member of the cultural majority continues, even today, to benefit directly and indirectly from institutional racism and our shared legacy of discrimination and apartheid. In the secular public discourse on this subject, many white people have adopted the position that the current generation has done nothing to effect or perpetuate the continued socioeconomic disadvantage of minority groups.

Although this may be true from a legalistic, secular perspective, it does not reflect the type of earnest repentance that Christ demands of His faithful followers. In order for the process of healing and unity between different racial, ethnic, and class groups to begin in earnest, those who have benefited, directly or indirectly, from our shared legacy of racial oppression must genuinely repent and seek forgiveness. Even if one has not actively oppressed racial minorities, it is still beneficial to repent as a means of acknowledging collective responsibility and initiating an earnest effort towards reconciliation.

The rapidly changing racial, ethnic, and class composition of the United States has ushered in many changes, both positive and negative. As Christians diligently seeking to apply ethical principles, the legacy of racism is one that must not be ignored. In order to ensure that the Christian church remains vital and relevant in the coming years, believers have an ethical responsibility to take proactive steps to begin a genuine process of reconciliation between racial and ethnic groups.

19. Ethics and Race

"We hold these truths to be self-evident,
that all men are created equal, that they are
endowed by their creator with certain inalienable rights,
that among these are life, liberty, and the pursuit of happiness"
U.S. Declaration of Independence

The words of the Declaration of Independence have been carefully chosen. The writers of this fundamental document labored over each word, aware of its significance to future generations. From their carefully crafted text we learn that our rights are not granted to us by our constitution or the system of government, but that these rights are ours from the moment we come into existence. All men are created equal. This is such a deceivingly simple statement. It is hard to understand why, to some of us, this truth is not as self-evident as the declaration of independence would lead us to believe. Our country has gone through endless struggles to make these words a reality. Each struggle has met with an equal and opposing force that chose an alternative, more convenient interpretation of the fundamental principle: that equality is meant to operate only when we are to be raised to an equal level to those above us, but it was hardly meant to equalize us with those below. Although it is easy for us to find fault with this obviously distorted argument, it is entirely another matter for us to put it into practice. It was hard for plantation owners to give up their human property that provided free labor in the nineteenth century. It was hard for school children to give up their territory and be forced to associate with those not of their own color. It is hard for politicians, businessman and professionals today to make room in their privileged ranks for people of different ethnicities. No matter how many barriers of race and discrimination are overcome, there are plenty out there still holding people back because of their ethnic background or the color of their skin. Even today, after so much ground has been gained, sometimes we see a successful minority businessman or government representative shine on an articulate argument in the media and we may catch ourselves involuntarily thinking something like "how about that!…not bad for a Latino…"

Racial discrimination has been my unwelcome lifetime companion. My first awareness of it came as a young boy, when I was forced to hurriedly leave my hometown and my family because of threats received when I purportedly failed to address a white shop-owner as "Sir". I remember a lonely, dull fear growing deep inside me, on the train leading me to unfamiliar lands, in the middle of the night. On this occasion as in many others, I encountered the flip side of human nature; an extraordinary life-saving kindness offered by total strangers. I was fortunate to have a relationship with God so I did not engender resentment or hatred in my heart. Instead, together with my wife, we have exercised our right to be treated equally, and resorted to civil disobedience on countless occasions. We were the first people of color to picket the McDonald's fast-food restaurant in Columbus, Missouri when they first opened in the early sixties. It was never our intention to embark on this crusade. We just meant to walk in and order hamburgers. And so we did, but we were then told that we could buy the hamburgers but that we could not eat them there. We simply said that if we were not welcome to eat them there, then we would just leave. We paid for the hamburgers but left them on the counter. We went back time and time again and the same thing happened. They would take our money, but they would not allow us to eat on the premises. One day, we decided not to leave. We sat down and calmly began to eat our hamburgers like everyone else in the restaurant (everyone else happened to be white of course). The manager hurriedly came over and asked us to leave immediately. We said we would, as soon as we were finished. He called the police. By the time the officer arrived, we had finished our meal and no arrests were made. I told other blacks what happened, and tried to get them to join us. They expressed their admiration but were too afraid to participate. We finally found support in a group of black students, who peacefully went back to the restaurant with us to assert our right to enjoy our meal. After a number of humiliating scenes at the restaurant, an order finally came down directly from headquarters to allow blacks to eat inside. This felt like sweet victory to me. We had gained this ground without resorting to violence of any sort, on either side of the dispute. Through an inner peaceful but strong resolution, we won many victories, big and small. We fought our battle of integration in barbershops, restaurants, schools, hotels and swimming pools. All along, I felt God's hand guiding us, protecting us. Others have not been so fortunate; many have given up their lives in the struggle. Some victims of discrimination harbor strong violent emotions against their oppressors, and find it impossible to shake them off. I have witnessed the silent wrath that festers in their hearts. I still see it in their eyes today. I wish I could write about these matters in the past tense, congratulating our collective selves for conquering racism. I cannot. Professor Cornell West, of Harvard and Princeton Universities Black Studies programs, said in his book "Race Matters" that racism is still alive and well in America today. I have to concur. Racism is the byproduct of an inordinate and unfounded fear. We fear anything that is not like us, any difference that we cannot explain. Whenever I have encountered racial discrimination, there is a group of people behind it that feel threatened and react with violent emotions. They may feel their territory or their privileges threatened. They may fear for their children, and how racial integration might affect or influence them. There is usually a dominant group feeling threatened by a minority. In my personal experiences, the dominant group was white and the minority was formed by underprivileged blacks. The blacks wished to have access to better homes, schools, jobs. The whites were filled with fear of losing their privilege to the blacks. And so the self-perpetuating friction continues. These were all Christian, God-fearing people. Not one of them could honestly say that equality was not a worthy idea. In spite of knowing that they are supposed to love each other and treat each other as they would like to be treated in turn, the deep unreasonable fear would take over. Hatred slowly simmered in their hearts until it reached boiling point in unlikely ways. A dispute over who could sit where in the bus could spill over to violent wars of words or physically violent clashes. A relatively small number of people instigated these outbursts. The larger number just followed out of a misplaced sense of loyalty not to let down the members of their own race. Which brings me to the subject of personal responsibility.

During the trial of an infamous war criminal of the Nazi regime during W.W. II, the judge posed a poignant question to the accused. The role of the accused officer during the Third Reich had been purely administrative. He had been in charge of logistics and transportation of prisoners to the concentration camps. His job was to assure that these tasks were carried out in a precise, timely manner, optimizing speed and efficiency. I believe the particulars of the case are public knowledge so there is no need for me to expand on the nature of the atrocities committed during that time at the Nazi concentration camps. Higher efficiency in logistics had a direct bearing on the number of people that would reach their final destination faster and at a lower cost to the war machine. The question the judge asked was if at any time during the systematic extermination of Jewish people, had the accused posed to himself the possibility of refusing to carry out orders and stop his individual involvement in the killing. The response came weakly. The accused stated that he had, in fact, agonized over the matter continuously. The alternative he faced was either to ignore the call of his conscience saying that there was nothing he could do about it, and that the slaughter would continue anyway, with or without his help; or to stand up for his ethical values and face the inevitable personal consequences. He chose the former. He continued to carry out orders in the most efficient manner possible, until the end of the war. His lack of personal responsibility cost uncounted numbers of innocent lives, including many children. Consider the alternative for a moment. Had he (and others with equivalent responsibilities) refused to enforce the monstrous orders, the outcome would have been much different. Our world today would not be bearing the scar of the Holocaust.

As we learn from these sad lessons of history, let us apply them to our own lives and take personal responsibility for our actions. It may not be that our weaknesses will directly cause loss of lives, but they will certainly cause somebody inordinate pain or make someone think that their worth is less because of the color of their skin, or their facial features. I grew up facing these aggressions, sometimes subtly, sometimes very directly. For years as a child I was made to believe that there was something wrong with me. If I heard people say that blacks had an offensive odor, I would wash with the strongest soap I could find. If I heard that people said that blacks were lazy, I would work three times as hard as an ordinary employee. Ultimately however, there was nothing I could do to measure up, because no matter how hard I tried there was one thing I could not do: I could not turn myself white. Many people defied the stigma and extended their hands to me. Other people would only show kindness when they were sure no one was watching. There should not be room for racism in the heart of a Christian. Whenever we fail to speak up in the face of an injustice, we are passively discriminating. We may appease our own conscience by saying that our words won't make a difference. We may say that it is up to politicians, lawmakers and the justice system to handle these matters; and that these situations will always occur, with or without our participation. Does this sound familiar? Next time you are tempted to appease your conscience that way, remember the question the judge posed to the war criminal and be ready to stand up and take bold personal responsibility for your actions.

I find great solace and inspiration in the passage of Peter and Cornelius in Acts 10. Cornelius is a Roman centurion. Peter is a Jew, and it is against the law of his people to associate with a Gentile. Both Cornelius and Peter are confronted with a vision eventually leading to their reluctant meeting. Cornelius seeks Peter and has him brought before him. Peter proceeds to relate the life of Jesus and offer witness to His miracles. When the Holy Spirit descends on the gentiles assembled in the audience, the Jewish believers are astonished to see the spirit being pored over the gentiles. Until then, they had thought this privilege was reserved only to people of their own nation. But Peter understood and rejoiced in the realization that God shows no favoritism and accepts men from every race, as long as they open their hearts to Him and bring Him into their lives.

It was my relationship with God that carried me through when I was discriminated against. It is God that will carry us on to a higher plane of understanding and love, whenever we are tempted to fall into the endless darkness of hatred or revenge.

Gender, nationality and race are perhaps the most significant circumstances that will shape the life of an individual from the very beginning. Of these three, race is the one quality that is most likely to affect his or her choices and circumstances. Many laws have been passed in the United States designed to bring an end to discrimination of all kinds. Racism poses very complex dynamics that tend to defy traditional ethical considerations. Affirmative action alone will not do it. It lowers the bar by providing an opportunity to minority candidates just because of their race, potentially overlooking more qualified candidates. It works as a temporary patch over situations where discrimination had been rampant. But it has the potential of alienating the groups who see their opportunity for advancement snatched away by what they perceive as an arbitrary selection process. Furthermore, it makes those groups who are in opposition dig their heels even deeper on any ground that has been left untouched by this measure, creating an even more unbalanced playing field for minorities. Political correctness can be misleading. For example, finding a new term to define the black race and calling it African-American can make us feel more comfortable dancing around the issue without getting at the root of the matter. The problem is we may inadvertently be swapping a "new and improved" term and causing the older term to turn into a racial slur. I believe it is better to address the essence of the issue rather than its form. Finding a more acceptable name for a problem is not the same as finding its solution. Violence is certainly not the answer either. You can't extinguish a flame with fire. Violence is a self-perpetuating calamity. Generation after generation pass their emotional wounds on to the next. Until it reaches a point where nobody really remembers what exactly they are fighting for. But every time they try to stop, the balance is so precarious that a simple misunderstanding or an isolated act of violence can bring the battle to a froth all over again. The bridges that need to be laid down need to be built stone by stone, with fierce consistency and perseverance. Every action, every word, need to come from a sincere humility of the heart. Charity is a quality that men either have or they have not, it is not dictated by race or ethnic origin. A worthy goal is to build these bridges so that anyone, on either side of it, can reach out and embrace the complexity of their neighbors. Only when we are able to do unto others as we would have them do unto us will be able to overcome those barriers and see that, in our fallible humanity, we are much more alike than dissimilar. Only then will the truths in the declaration of independence become self-evident. In our strife to find an ethical path for our lives, we need only to look at the life of Jesus to guide us through the darkest passages. Only when we are able to recognize and take to our hearts the basic teaching of Jesus Christ do we have any hope of redemption: to love our neighbor as we love ourselves. To love each other as He loves us.

20. Ethics and Work

"Because I helped to wind the clock,
I come to hear it strike."
William Butler Yeats

At the conclusion of a sermon I delivered some years entitled "Your Job Matters to God", a high profile member of my church came up to me and said:

"Pastor, that was a splendid message you just delivered. I only wish that the people who need it the most could have been here to hear it."

This well-meaning remark actually troubled me. I thought about it for days on end. I realized that sermons affect people in different ways, but I had never intended to target a particular audience with a message. I still don't to this day. I decided to listen to my taped sermon again, and go over my notes carefully. After reviewing the sermon several times and praying to understand, it became clear to me that the message had really hit home very powerfully with the member who made the remark, and one way she found of easing the powerful effect of it was to deflect some of its impact to those who were not present. A sort of "sermon overflow valve". I will recreate here the salient points of that sermon.

Your job matters to you, your family and your circle of friends and acquaintances. What you do also matters to your clients, your vendors, and your colleagues. But there is someone else to whom your job is very important: God. Yes, your job matters to God. It matters to God that you give a full day's work for a full day's pay. In some job situations, your every minute is monitored. You need to punch in and out even if you are taking a short break. In other environments, you are paid the same amount of money whether you are working all the time or not. It is in fact an ethical challenge to fulfill your time obligations when no one is controlling your performance. But whatever your work environment may be, it is ultimately up to you to make sure that you are not only prompt and punctual but that you give your best during the time that you are working. Maintain your integrity even when others have incorporated certain "flexibility" in their schedules as common practice. As a young employee in a highly supervised environment I observed my coworkers reduce their actual work hours by a few minutes here and there. They would get their belongings ready before they actually punched out. Those last ten minutes could certainly not be considered work. But what harm would it do? Then there were frequent trips to the restroom, or sneaking away to a quiet corner for a brief catnap. I also noticed that whenever we were waiting for an assignment or for new instructions, it was easy to let ourselves go and fall into idle conversation as if we were on our own personal time. In fact, there were many other productive things we could be doing, such as cleaning up our area or finding ways to improve our productivity. We were getting paid for those minutes. Although it may seem harsh or unrealistically strict, this basic ethical principle will keep you out of trouble. It will also give you a sense of pride in your work. Without it, you are not likely to ever achieve a true sense of satisfaction in your job.

The same applies to the myriad of little self-appointed job perks that we find so harmless. We don't think twice about using our office phone to make personal calls. We browse the Internet to shop for personal items. We take home office supplies (it's just a pen!). If your employer has explicitly allowed these privileges, then it is absolutely fine to enjoy them. In most cases, however, the employer has placed these items in your care for the performance of your function. Any use that is not strictly related to your work constitutes an abuse of your employer's trust. This issue of trust is sometimes not readily evident. It is easy to picture your employer when you work in a small operation. You probably meet him or her on a regular basis, and it is possible that your employer hired you directly. It is more difficult to personify your employer when you are one of thousands of employees in a huge corporation. At some point, even in a large organization, your employer had a job that needed doing and trusted you to do it. This is the trust relationship I am referring to. This ethical principle applies to big and small work environments, just the same. Let's assume you work as a clerk in a dry-cleaning store in a small town. It is just you and the hard working owner who is struggling to make ends meet. You are an honest employee, you would never think of taking money from the cash register. But how about that hospitality candy on the counter? Although the owner intends it for customers, it must surely be acceptable for you to have some. Surely you can't be expected to have that candy in front of your eyes all day and not reach out for one small piece? And how about putting a bunch of candy in your pocket for the drive home? How much is too much? Avoid the trap of thinking that it is ethical as long as you don't get caught! Here is a rule of thumb whenever you are in doubt; anything that you are considering doing while you are not being watched, anything that you could not feel absolutely comfortable doing just as well in the presence of your boss or employer is most probably unethical.

Sick and personal days are another area where we find justification for bending the rules. Personal days are usually not carried over to the following year. This means that if you don't use them before the cut-off date, you lose them. The same applies to your sick days. The problem is that these are not days given to you to use as you see fit. These are days that your employer has incorporated into your employment contract to allow for unforeseen circumstances. If you have not faced any such circumstance, then you are both healthy and fortunate, but you are not entitled to the days off. The use of these days for any other reason is, again, a breach of your employer's trust. God expects you to be honest in your job, don't let Him and yourself down. Be honest in your deeds and in your words. Avoid gossip for it not only wastes your time but also is both hurtful and destructive… and this was the message in my sermon. It addressed the more practical or measurable aspects of work. But there is more to work ethics than this.

The right man can turn any job into a good job. And any job can be done with dignity and pride or with indifference. In my experience workers fall into one of three categories; those who do as little as possible in order to get by, those who do only what they were supposed to do and no more, and finally those happy people who do their absolute best.

Moreover, there is one very special kind of worker, who becomes an inspiration to others and often encourages others to do their work cheerfully and well. These workers are a treasure to themselves and their colleagues. Their work truly honors God. Their attitude is contagious and engages others in a positive and constructive way. They do not engage in gossip, they are honest and they produce excellent work. This does not necessarily mean that they work longer hours or that they continue to work into their own personal time. They find joy in their work. Their peers and superiors usually respect them. They see beyond the daily routine and look to their jobs as a piece in the giant puzzle of God's plan for them. They rejoice in a sense of accomplishment. They apply to their work as a vehicle to become better stewards of Christ. This sounds extremely desirable; you might think, but is it possible for anyone (other than saints) to achieve such state of grace in their jobs? Absolutely.

First of all, we need to get rid of the notion that our spiritual life and our worldly occupation belong in two separate planes. We are Christians all the time, 24 hours a day, seven days a week. In fact, work is one of the places where the dynamics of human interaction boil right up to the surface. People of different socioeconomic levels, of different cultures, races and faiths are all thrown together in one place. It is precisely the place to exercise our spiritual muscles to the fullest. Every day has the potential to offer lessons in compassion, humility, integrity and patience. Once we understand this, the rest is easy. Regardless of whoever signs our paycheck, we are first and foremost full time Christian workers. This does not mean that you will attempt to impose your faith in the workplace. Rather you will allow the shining light of Christ to reflect on your work and your attitude towards your coworkers and your employer. Your stewardship can take many forms. In my case it is very easy. It is most natural for people to accept that a Pastor is a Christian worker. But what about a doctor, a technician, a post-office clerk? They are Christian workers too, just as much as a pastor. All they need to do is to offer their work to God in prayer, and ask in return for God to guide their hands, so that they will work in the manner that will honor and glorify Him.

Think of Jesus, the ultimate Christian worker. What was the one constant of his work on this earth? Service. He did not ask to be served; he made it very clear that his life was devoted to serve his Father. Once we consider that our work is our means to serve others, much of the weight is lifted off our shoulders. And once we consider that our work is ultimately our offering to God, and he is there beside us every minute of every day, the rest of the burden just melts away.

We become fulltime Christians, at work. Our life is no longer divided into spiritual hours and work hours. Our life is one, joyful and sincere service to our Lord. Surely there will be difficult times; people will get on our nerves, equipment will conspire against us, but we can go back to our center by finding God in our challenges.

The most interesting aspect of this attitude is that it will trigger a wonderful domino effect that will surprise you. The seeds that you sow will flourish in unexpected places. It may require time and consistency of purpose; particularly if you work in a culture of complaint and minimal effort. It is up to you to become the catalyst of change. Once you achieve a work environment where everybody truly pulls together as one for the company to grow and prosper, everyone benefits. The example you set for others could very well become the pillar for the success of your employer.

Work ethics don't stop when we leave the workplace. What you say about your employer among your friends or in casual conversation has an impact too. Be mindful of your words. This also applies after you no longer work for that employer. There may be times when you do not agree with your employer's policies or practices. Unless these practices are illegal, in which circumstance you would have an obligation to society to report them to the proper authorities, you would do best to keep your grievances private. Bring them forward only in their proper forum, and only with those directly concerned. Your understandable impact to vent your frustration will ultimately bring no good to you, and it might hurt the company and those people who are still working there. Furthermore, it is a poor reflection on your character, and any potential employer that might consider hiring you could be wary of becoming the object of your derisive comments should something displease you about your new job.

While we are on the subject or work ethics let me propose this fundamental guideline to you; the first ethical principle to be followed related to your work is to be true to yourself. We are fortunate to live in a country that affords choices and opportunities. Find a career that is true to your heart and vocation. So many of us feel stuck in our jobs. We decide to stay for different reasons. There may be health or family circumstances, or others may be dependent on us for their subsistence. These life situations are very real and understandable.

The burden can become heavy indeed, until we begin to feel chained to the present circumstances. Is this happening to you? Keep working towards your goal of finding a job where you can develop fully as a person. In some cases this will require that you change careers. In other cases, however, it just requires that you alter your approach to the job you already have. If you are facing financial constraints, there are multiple sources of career counseling and continuing education geared towards your needs. Your opportunity is waiting. You spend long hours at our jobs, and it is up to you to find the best place for your talents. Fill your life with purpose and hope, so that you can become the master of your days instead of their servant.

Start today - right now! You already know what it takes to have an ordinary day at work. Now turn it into something extraordinary.

21. Ethics and Stewardship

"We make a living by what we get,
we make a life by what we give."
Winston Churchill

As I was reflecting on the subject of this chapter, I reviewed the definition of stewardship that I had presented over thirty years ago in my capacity as Associate Director of the Division of World Mission Support of the American Baptist Churches. I am not able to improve on it; I find that it still applies today. I defined stewardship as the management of responsibility in all aspects of our lives, including talent, time and resources. I grant equal importance to each of these three areas. Stewardship is most often mentioned in relation to money or financial resources. It is not limited to this area alone. Money is just one part of a three-part equation. We have much more to give than money. In fact, to those of us who find ourselves in a comfortable financial situation, it might be more difficult to give our time than our money. On the other hand, for people who are not able to give money, the opportunities are there to contribute their special skills or to support charitable endeavors with their time. Be it time, skill or money, our ability or willingness to give is connected to our management of these three areas of our lives in all their multiple facets. I am often amazed by some people who give of their time generously and I find they are usually the busiest. They have jobs, children, homes, families. Yet they manage to assign the proper time to each, without ever being hurried or out of breath. It occurs to me that these people never question if they have the time to do it. After all, we all have the same amount of time, 24 hours in a day, 7 days in a week and so forth. It is what we do with our time that makes the difference. It is the value we apply to different activities that sets the priority of how much time will be allotted to them. If our charitable contribution of time will have to wait until everything we must do or wish to do is exhausted, then we most probably will not find the time to do much for others. If on the other hand, we consider that our time is not our own but was given to us by God in the first place, and can be taken away from us just as well, the perceived use of it in the service of God takes on an entirely different perspective. It is almost as if the only time we get to keep is the time we give away for others.

Our stewardship is intimately linked to the commitments we make to others and the degree to which we honor these commitments. In fact, Jesus would have us know that the real test of the sincerity of the commitment that we have made to Him is expressed by what we do for the least fortunate people in our society. Jesus does not stop there. He also warns us that the failure to make a commitment is as harmful a development of proper stewardship as is breaking a commitment that you have already made. It is a sin of omission. In Mathew 25: 31-46 Jesus teaches us that at the time of judgment, we will not only be judged by what we have given to those in need but also by the needs that we have ignored or not acted upon; "...whatever you did not do for one of the least of these, you did not do for me." Let your imagination run wild for just a moment and picture coming face to face with Jesus. Let's say you are doing your shopping in the grocery store, and there he is, ahead of you in the checkout line. Yep. He turns around, introduces himself, and you know: it's Him. As you push your heavy cart full of groceries you notice that His cart is empty. What would you do? Would you ask Him if he would like to get some food, or something to drink? Would you invite him to your home and offer him a good meal and a warm bed to sleep in? Or would you look the other way, change lanes and pretend you didn't notice? Wouldn't you feel a little guilty and just a tad nervous if you didn't help Jesus? Let's face it, here He is, the Son of God, who will be sitting at the right hand of the Father at the time of your judgment to put in a good word for you. You wouldn't dare ignore Him. Well, it so happens that this is exactly what you are doing when you ignore the least of your brothers. At least that is the way Jesus told us He would consider it, just as if you were ignoring Jesus himself. Jesus leaves no room for apathy toward the hungry, the orphans, the widows, those imprisoned, sick and afflicted, the homeless and the oppressed. Whatever excuses we can come up with are simply unacceptable to Him. Christians are called to action, called to serve others. Answering this call sometimes comes easily, as in the case of a newborn child, a new spouse or a new job. But within the framework of Christian ethics, stewardship makes no distinction as to the object of our commitment or the need for it. Just as we are eager to show our love for those near and dear to us, we must be just as willing to show mercy to those who are far and distanced from us by virtue of their circumstances. True stewardship calls for an ethical balance of love, judgment and mercy where we welcome all people equally, whatever the circumstances. Even if the cause is not fashionable or politically correct, stewardship calls us to act and to give, irregardless.

As a Christian steward, receive your gifts gratefully and use them joyfully and responsibly. Take stock of your God given gifts, and offer them in service to those who need them. If you have the desire to give, but don't know where to start, think of your Church as your training ground. It might be that your skills could be of use in your Church during the service. Offer your help. Are you handy with tools? Offer your help with facilities or maintenance. Can you cook? Can you boil water? Offer you help with the hospitality in your Parish. Sometimes a cup of coffee and a kind word is all a person needs to get through a rough day. Once you have found your footing in familiar surroundings, spread your wings and expand beyond your Church, engage in community service. If you feel lost or don't know where to help, start anywhere and just keep trying until you find one that fits your skills. God will guide you to where you can serve Him best. And don't be miserly with your time, it is just as valuable as your money and skills. Most important of all, keep your promises.

The large majority of people are naturally generous. Our attitude towards our material possessions has a spiritual dimension, it is part of our relationship with God. Our material possessions require a great deal of our effort to obtain, and thereafter a great deal of our attention to maintain. Money has not only become a pagan god to many people, but asking for money in some cases even becomes taboo in Church. Parishioners shift uncomfortable in their seats when the sermon from the pulpit addresses their pockets. Some will self-righteously proclaim that such matters do not belong in a spiritual setting. I find that these people react this way because they are the most affected by the sermon. They know that they are not fulfilling their promise. They are aware that they are not putting God first in their lives, and are not giving commensurate to the abundance of gifts that they have received. Whenever I hear these critics I am reassured that the message indeed hit the target, and even needs to be repeated more often. We need to be reminded that God expects us to manage our treasures responsibly. If asked for advice on good stewardship, I simply resort to basic good management principles: stay out of debt, refrain from extravagance, and be generous. Fairly simple guidelines, but quite a challenge to follow. When Jesus was asked by a rich man what was the way to eternal life, he received the one reply he did not want to hear (Mark 10:21): "Go, sell everything you have and give it to the poor, and you will have treasure in heaven." Neither of us really wants to hear this, there must be another way to do it! Give everything up that we have worked so hard to accumulate! It is unthinkable! But the message is not ambiguous and is not left open to interpretation. We are fortunate to live in a nation of unparalleled wealth. Americans have access to more creature comforts than ever before, and we quickly grow accustomed to these comforts. We hoard and accumulate, we save and invest, and we set aside a share to give to charity. But when the economy takes a downswing, charity is the most expendable item on our budget planning. Blame unemployment, war, and the bear market. We look at our finances and decide there is no way that we can keep up our standard of living at this rate. Something has to give, meaning, we will give less. But for the poor, for those in the deepest need, the economy always stays the same. There is never enough to go around. Where the next meal will come from is not certain. The possibility of losing the roof over their heads is a daily threat. Every day they wake up hungry, cold, or sick. All they have to look forward to is another day of deprivation. I propose to you that when finances get tighter for you, they are probably getting tighter for many others who are in a far more precarious position. This is the time to rethink your expenses and find ways to give more. To that individual who you may never meet, that is being pushed over the cruel edge of poverty today, your gift is the line that sustains life for one more precious day. Your offering becomes their warm blanket tonight or their bus money to get to their job interview tomorrow. Is there anything you can do to alter their fate? Is there room for Jesus at your table?

In Mathew 22, Jesus tells us of a thought-provoking parable. The king's son was getting married and the king invited his guests to a plentiful banquet. But the guests refused to come. The enraged king sent his army to destroy the ungrateful guests, and sent his servants to bring to the wedding all the people they could find in the village. But when the king was at the banquet he noticed a guest that was not wearing wedding clothes. He had him thrown out; "for many are invited, but few are chosen." Through this many-layered parable we learn at least two main lessons. First we are told that we have been invited to the kingdom of God, and we need to be grateful and heed the invitation joyfully for He has taken great troubles in preparing a plentiful feast for us. Additionally, we are told that when invited, we need to pay the proper respect that the circumstances require, and show with our actions that we care to be deserving of the honor. If we are to engage in stewardship according to the teachings of Jesus, we must make sure that we are dressed for the wedding. We must be prepared to change personally, into our best spiritual clothes, and rise to the occasion. We must seek to alter the lives of those around us so that they will too have a chance to attend the banquet. It occurs to me that there is a third underlying wake-up call in this parable: the invitation can come at any time, and we need to be ready. And we need to make sure that our village is ready for the banquet as well. As a nation, Americans are blessed with abundance and riches. As good stewards of these gifts, we must exercise responsible citizenship and make sure that our leaders know our priorities. We can be more generous, less wasteful. We can reach out even further to other nations who are less fortunate and offer our resources, our skills, and dedicate a portion of our time to these causes. The time is overdue for our nation to rededicate its resources for the purpose for which it was founded. It was founded to be free, but free for a purpose. This purpose being that others can be freed in turn from their own chains of illiteracy, malnutrition, illness, or social inequality. By reaching out to those impoverished nations, we earn our right, as a nation, to sit at the wedding banquet as an honored guest.

I think of stewardship whenever I hear the evangelical question that is posed to people so often: "Brother/Sister, are you saved?" I heard it as a young boy many times, and I knew what the question meant. It was meant to inquire if I had been saved from my guilt, my sin, my eternal damnation. But it always occurred to me that a second question should follow the first – that is – what are you saved for? Jesus roundly answered that question for us. We are saved in order to serve. To serve responsibly, giving equally of our time, talent and treasure.

22. Ethics and Spiritual Leadership

"Some people grow under responsibility, others merely swell."
Carl Hubbel

The Pastor of a Church is a professional called by God to be the spiritual overseer of a congregation. This function is performed under a variety of names: Father, Reverend, Pastor, Elder, Minister and many others. In this chapter, I will use the term Pastor to refer to all of these in general, and will take the license to refer the Pastor as "him" to include both male and female. I am writing from a Christian perspective, since this is the path I have chosen in my own life. I believe, however, that the guiding principles of ethics discussed here apply to spiritual leaders from all faiths.

As I said, the Pastor receives a call by God to serve his flock. How does the Pastor recognize this call? You may have heard accounts of lightning bolts and booming voices coming from above, but for many it does not come in such an earth-shattering manner. The call can be gentle, persistent, and come when we least expect it. Some Pastors have a strong vocation that starts early in their lives. Others are people that followed different careers and were called to make a mid-life change in their lives and follow the new path that God set before them. Whichever way the call comes, becoming a Pastor is a decision that requires a great deal of reflection and courage. It is not a job to be taken lightly, as it carries the weight of responsibility over the spiritual life of many others. Becoming a Pastor may not be a popular choice of careers with family members or friends, who may feel left behind. And yet, when God calls, the heart follows. Although every believer is in a way a minister (servant) of God, those who have been called to a special ministry to become Pastors bear a greater responsibility for doing much more than would otherwise be expected of them.

As professionals, Pastors undertake a threefold ethical commitment: a commitment to those they serve, the individual members of the parish; a commitment to other colleagues in their profession; and a commitment to the profession of the ministry itself. A Pastor is expected to be fairer than fair and wiser than wise. The minister is called to bring the teachings of Christ to life, and turn into a living example for the community. Is this fair? Is this even possible? The duties of a Pastor require that the standards of morality laid out in the Bible be followed all the time, in every aspect of the Pastor's life. Is this a reasonable expectation? It is only possible and fair and reasonable through God. A Pastor cannot conduct his duty relying solely on his own will or strength. A ministry has not been given to him because he deserves it, but because it is God's plan. It is the Pastor's job to stay out of his own way and allow God to carry out His divine purpose through him. He must strive to keep that direct line with God connected 24/7. Even if he may sometimes stumble, a sincere ministry will ultimately reflect God's shining love on his congregation.

A Pastor gets to wear many hats. He is at different times either teacher, critic, cheerleader, motivator, manager, friend, writer, counselor or entrepreneur. It is a delicate balance to fulfill all these roles and not to overstep any ethical boundaries. Pastors should be careful to make sure that what they say is true and that there is verifiable evidence to support the claim if necessary. If he fails to assert his credibility among the people in his congregation, it is unlikely that they will tune in to his message with an open mind. The cloud of doubt will tint even the words that come directly from the Scriptures. Confidentiality is a quality that the Pastor must guard with the utmost zeal. A Pastor should always warn the potential confessor that he does not need to reveal any confidential information. It is always a good precaution to find out if this information which he is about to receive has been shared with anyone else. Let the confessor know that confidentiality is precarious when a confidence has been revealed to more than one person. In case of a breach, the confessor could never be certain of who is responsible for it. Whenever the Pastor receives a confidence, he is ethically bound to keep it. Are there any special circumstances that would warrant the breach of such trust? Yes. A Pastor can break a confidence if he considers the confessor to be a threat to himself, to others, if the confidence is of a severe criminal nature, or if there is a possibility that anyone is about to take their own life. If a Pastor is ever in a position requiring him to breach the secrecy of a confession, he should make absolutely certain that the circumstances unequivocally justify such an extreme course of action.

The Pastor should match only the skills he has with the needs of his flock. When in doubt, the Pastor should let it be known that he does not have the answer at hand and make every effort to research the matter and find an answer. If the issue is greater than the skills or time available, then it is fit to refer to a trained professional who can expertly deal with the case in hand. A Pastor who overextends the reach of his expertise in order to impress his followers is doing his community a grave disservice.

The Pastor needs always to be acutely aware of the ramifications and consequences of his actions and words. He not only needs to be ethical but to also keep the appearance of it. Financial matters are of a particularly sensitive nature. The pressure to raise funds and comply with the goals and objectives of the Church can cloud the judgment of how ethical the methods being employed are. The same goes for the way in which the funds are being spent. All methods and transactions are best conducted transparently, or not at all. Though it might be hard to turn away from a potentially lucrative opportunity, it will be harder down the line to face public scrutiny without the ability to clearly document and report on the financial activity that is under review. If there was ever a shortcut to career suicide, neglect of a Pastor's financial duties is surely it.

A Pastor's words have the power to heal, influence, guide, encourage and warn. The words in his sermons are perhaps those that will have the most immediate and recognizable effect on the larger number of his congregation. Three tools are at hand: prayer, reflection and preparation. There is danger in stepping behind the pulpit unprepared. To begin with, the Pastor is indulging in the waste of other people's time. Members of the church make an effort to attend the service. They take time for God, making preparations at home, organizing their other commitments, maybe even dressing especially for the occasion. At the proper time, they all look up to the pulpit, each with their own troubles, their own expectations. They open their hearts to the message that will help them find God's way in their lives. And then the Pastor lets them all down perhaps pretending that, although he did have a message prepared beforehand, the Lord told him to preach about something else. He starts to improvise. The

Pastor knows he is telling a lie. Furthermore, some members of the congregation may even be moved by the fact that the minister is being spoken to directly by God and pay extra-careful attention to these irresponsible words. Imagine that you are going out to dinner to an upscale gourmet restaurant, renown for its unsurpassed Clam Chowder. You go through the usual routine: call in a reservation, get dressed, locate the address, and find a parking spot. Your mouth is watering as you are seated at your very fine table. But when the chowder arrives, you are informed that it came straight from a can, because the Chef didn't have time to cook. And to make the insult worse, they intend to charge the full price anyway. What would you think of the integrity of this restaurant? Whenever a Pastor gives an improvised sermon, he is serving his congregation canned chowder; and he is not even admitting to it. Were it a misdemeanor to lie, then it would be a felony to mislead a trusting follower of Christ. A great sermon is not based upon the preacher's desire to impress the audience with his oratorical ability or with the fertility of his imagination. It is based upon the biblical and ethical teachings of the Scriptures. People who come to worship have only a passing concern for the intellectual details of history, whether factual or distorted. They come to worship a true and living God. They thirst to be told about how He is working in this world today, and hunger to understand how to apply what they are hearing in their own lives. It is cheating the congregation of its rightful opportunity for a Pastor to offer a sermon that merely pacifies and entrances the crowd, rather than one that glorifies the Lord. To seek to entertain rather than challenge is akin to the type of church music that lifts the body out of the pew but not the soul out of its pit of despair. There is room to interpret the Gospel with inspiration from the Holy Spirit, but this in no way gives the Pastor license to manipulate people into believing that what they are hearing comes directly from the Lord. Additionally, the Pastor must be truthful in all things, not least in crediting the source of his ideas. There is a thin line between plagiarism and authentic research. No one person can be completely original. What we have heard or read before inevitable blends into our own thoughts. But materials taken directly from another author need to be properly credited. One unethical action from the pulpit, even if the whole congregation is a willing participant, screams louder than a thousand sermons.

The essential ministry of the Pastor is the spiritual nourishment of his flock. He must tend to his flock daily, constantly. There is no leave of absence or vacation time in this job. The Pastor is always on duty, to help his people find a way out of darkness and teach them the joy of living as a Christian. Joy is commonly equated with happiness but they are in essence quite different. Happiness can be bestowed by anyone, on anyone. Joy can only be bestowed by Christ. On the flip side, happiness can be taken away, but there is no force powerful enough to take away God's joy from the heart of a Christian.

Sadly, there are times when things don't go so joyfully. A Pastor might be forced to face the reality that the parish he is serving is not a parish he would wish to belong to as a member of the congregation. This Pastor may be faced with one of the most difficult decisions in his career. It may be that the members of the church who have the most influence or financial power are steering the parish down a road that diverges from true Christian teachings. The Pastor needs to carefully evaluate if he should make every attempt to correct this situation before even thinking of leaving. There are times when small groups of influential members of the congregation start taking over the role of the Pastor. They may just attempt to direct smaller matters such as office hours or music choices, but they may further encroach on to critical matters and even attempt to direct the content of the sermons. All this might start innocently, as a casual objection to a particular subject or treatment in a particular sermon. There is just a short step from harmless objection to veiled censorship. If a Pastor is put in an untenable situation, he may have to break away from this congregation and leave. The question to ask himself when he is debating with this decision is: if Christ were to come to town today, would he visit this Church? A Pastor's duty is to every member of his community, not to a select privileged group of individuals. Once every alternative course of action has been exhausted and the decision has been made, the separation needs to be done in as ethical a manner as possible. A Pastor should never seek to be divisive or to participate in gossip only to protect himself or his reputation. He should be discreet and not air publicly his differences.

He may find that other people approach him to support an opposing faction to the divisive group. The Pastor must make sure that he does not indulge in forming his own personal fan club. His main concern is the integrity and health of the faith community. At the same time, he must make sure that he is not running away from issues just to keep the peace. That would be just as unethical as staying. Any grievances that are serious enough to provoke his separation from his flock should be properly dealt with within the group of people directly responsible. Thereafter, once the Pastor has left, he should sever all professional contact with that church. Although it may be tempting to act in a self-righteous manner and seek those who agree with him to follow him to a new venue, he should be mindful of the real motivation for such actions. He needs to question his true motives, and rule out any personal gain, pride or desire to control. The community would do well to heal itself and find its way to God under the leadership of a new Pastor, who may be able to find new ways to lead them to the light. It would be unethical for the Pastor to take any further action at this point, except to pray that the congregation is able to find its true way to Christ.

If you are about to embark on a career as a Pastor, or if you have received God's call and you are considering the ministry, I would like to leave you with the beautiful words of Mathew 5:16 "…let your light shine before men, that they may see your good deeds and praise your Father in heaven."

23. Ethics and Self-Responsibility

"The last temptation is the greatest treason:
to do the right deed for the wrong reason."
T.S. Eliot

We have arrived to the very core of ethics: the distinction between right and wrong. In order for us to walk confidently, we must first be able to clearly distinguish the shadows from the light. For most of us this distinction becomes a lifelong struggle. We have a hunger to live our lives with integrity and in order to do this we must be have an inner compass that will guide our decisions and actions. Even when we think that we have a good grip on the subject, a new situation arises that challenges our hard-earned notions.

Have you ever watched one of those current affairs TV debates? First you hear the argument on one side and you end up fairly convinced that clearly, this is the objective point of view, and then the opposing argument is presented and you are back where you started. You were hardly aware that a simple event could be looked at from so many angles. In a legal battle, the judge will ultimately be the one to determine on the legality of an issue. Who is to say whether an action is ethically right or wrong? And are we to be ethical for fear of judgment or should ethical behavior be its own reward? In some form or other we all belong to a group. Even those who stand by themselves, as independent thinkers, are affected by those who have gone before them. Influences are all around us, from our peers, our culture, the groups we belong to. To make it even more confusing, the popular perceptions of right and wrong can change over time. What was perfectly acceptable in the sixteenth century can be considered aberrant behavior today. So how are we to know what is ethical and what is not? How can we tell? Who sets the rules today?

Those of you who have children may be able to relate. When a child is told not to do something, it is not unusual for the child at some point to start asking why. And if the parent replies that the child should not do it because it is bad, the child might ask: says who? So how do we know if something is “bad”? What makes right “right” and wrong “wrong”? Says who?

As opposed to a legal confrontation in which a judge will ultimately determine the outcome, there is no tangible or visible sign to show us if what he have just done is ethical or not. The judge resides within us. The personal maintenance of ethicality is a central theme that you will find throughout this book.

The reason we struggle over ethical judgments is that we are our own defense attorney and prosecutor. Whenever we are in doubt about an action we attempt to reason with ourselves that perhaps what we are considering is not really wrong, it is just social convention that determined it so. So where is the initial determination made of what is right and wrong? Was the evolution of social standards upheld over time because they are useful to contain chaos, or are there independent standards that stand alone to survive scrutiny and analysis? The principles of ethics are universal and immutable. To claim that they are not would be to negate all that is good and decent in ourselves. It would be like watching a group of children playing under a light and mistaking the children with the shadows they project on the ground. The shadows would not exist without the children, but the children would continue to exist even if you turned off the light and the shadows were gone.

The distinction between right and wrong enables you to respond to your needs for internal harmony, as well as your needs for harmony with the outer world. Self-responsibility in turn allows you to begin taking on the challenge of ethics instead of surrendering that responsibility to others (i.e., loved ones, health professionals, spiritual experts, people in authority). Self-responsibility is the process of empowering yourself to become responsible for your own integrity. In our times, it is increasingly rare to find people assuming responsibility for their own actions. Whenever something goes wrong, as in the case of an accident or injury, the first instinct is to find who is to blame. Think of this as an example. I heard recently that if you are having a party at your home, and you serve alcoholic refreshments, you could, in some cases, be held liable for an incident that happens after the party if it can be proved that alcohol played a part in the accident. You would think that the responsibility would fall on the individual that consumed alcohol beyond his or her limit.

Not so. The legal system becomes increasingly convoluted as more and more people try to find more and more ways to get away from facing the consequences of their actions. Consequently, laws keep being revised to make these people accountable. It is a self-defeating mechanism.

I was very impressed once by a casual comment made by a well-respected Olympic medalist sailor. One fine afternoon he was sailing recreationally, with a group of friends. One inexperienced crewmember made an abrupt maneuver, and the expert sailor narrowly missed injuring his hand. When a concerned friend blamed the beginner saying he should have been more careful, the self-responsible sportsman simply said "I had my hand in the wrong place." This short statement revealed to me a great deal about the way his mind worked. His extraordinary self-awareness and balanced thinking is a big part of what makes him stand out as an athlete.

I find another paradox in the consumer trends popular today. Interestingly enough, there is a legal action being brought forward against a fast-food restaurant chain, pleading that their advertising is aimed at creating a compulsion in consumers that has resulted in their obesity. Please don't misunderstand my statement; I am not an advocate for the supplier. Far from it. The trouble I am having with the issue is that, even before the legal action made the news, I was aware that eating large quantities of fast food was not a healthy habit. Since I am not a healthcare expert with access to privileged information, it occurs to me that this knowledge is available to the average consumer. Tempting advertisements are very effective in leading us to a purchase, but is it not our choice after all? It would be an entirely different matter if the supplier concealed or withheld information that the product might be harmful. In that case, the consumer is indeed a victim of manipulation and has not been given the right to choose. Attempting to argue the legal merits of the case is better left to the experts; my intention here is to illustrate the point of self-responsibility. Assigning responsibility for your actions outside of yourself is comfortable and easy. It silences the conscience and allows us to proceed with all the other "important" things that clutter our daily lives. This kind of thinking will make it difficult for you to begin assuming responsibility for yourself, and to prepare yourself for the task of gaining and maintaining your integrity. Reality confronts us with rights and wrongs at every turn. Free will is a challenge. Having a choice is a tremendous responsibility. Our smallest action has repercussions on the lives of others. A decision made in a brightly lit boardroom can have devastating effects on an obscure little village in a foreign country. From the minimal decisions that we make every minute, all the way to the major essential matter of our salvation, at the end of the day it all boils down to our individual choices. There is no family or group salvation. There is no "soul-fitness" club that we can join. When a faith community receives divine blessings as a group, it is often the result of the individual prayers and labors of a few. Even in the Old Testament, where people are addressed generally as a nation, there is still a very particular personal accountability set out. Such is the mandate of the Ten Commandments.

We have wondered if ethical principles are a result of social convention or if they are independent standards that have developed over time. The third alternative is that ethical principles have been laid out for us by something outside of ourselves. Bigger than ourselves, in fact, and more perfect. Fortunately for us, there is a set of clear principles that have been given to us in the Bible, through the teachings of Jesus and in the examples he set for us through His words and actions. We not only have the Word of God to guide us, but also a role model that showed us how the Word was made flesh. He lived in our world, contended with our failures and temptations, and conquered His spirit to lead us into our salvation. All we have to do is follow these principles, and the rest of the work has already been done for us.

When a rich man came to Jesus an asked him what he could to have access to eternal life (Mathew 19: 16-21) Jesus replied:

"Why do you ask me about what is good? There is only One who is good. If you want to enter life, obey the commandments."

"Which ones?" the man inquired.

"Do not murder, do not commit adultery, do not steal, do not give false testimony, honor your mother and your father and love your neighbor as yourself."

"All these I have kept" the young man said, "What do I still lack?"

Jesus answered, "If you want to be perfect, sell your possessions and give to the poor, and you will have treasure in heaven. Then come, follow me."

Jesus gave us two very clear instructions: follow the commandments, and follow me. This is the way to a perfect spiritual existence. Restricted by our limitations and weakness, alas, we are far from perfect. But every step taken in the direction of following Jesus is a step in the right direction. And anything that takes us away from Him, is therefore, the wrong direction. So, in a nutshell, here is how we tell right from wrong. We received further education on the subject from the Apostle Paul, when he writes about the fruits of the spirit. "But the fruit of the Spirit is love, joy, peace, patience, kindness, goodness, faithfulness, gentleness and self-control. Against such things there is no law." (Galatians 5:22,23)

Wisely used the Fruit of the Spirit can lead us to reaching our potential in Christ and to becoming the complete person that God intends us to be. When a gift of such value is offered freely a wise person does not turn away and refuse it, rather they accept the gift in the spirit in which it was intended, and they cherish it. Whenever we are in doubt, or our inner moral compass fails us, it is fit to ask: does the action I am considering cultivate the fruits of the spirit? Does it bring me a step closer to Jesus or does it take me away from Him? With this guidance, you can walk confidently in the world, in the knowledge that you can indeed distinguish the shadows from the light. We are fortunate, as Christians, to have such clear answers to our question.

24. Ethics, Happiness and Joy

"I have come that they may have life,
and have it to the full."
John 10:10

For thousands of years, philosophers have been grappling with the concept of happiness. They have pondered on the nature of it, the pursuit of it, and its relationship to ethical conduct. Plato argued that ethics is the only way to happiness. Aristotle posed that a happy life can only be achieved through the repetition of morally right actions until they become habit.

The terms joy and happiness are generally used interchangeably. From a Christian Ethics perspective, I hereby wish to make an important distinction between the two. Observing this distinction makes it easier to understand the place and importance that both happiness and joy occupy in our lives.

If you ask any individual in the street what his ultimate goal in life is, you are likely to obtain the reply: "I want to be happy". Very well, but what does that mean in tangible terms? To me, happiness might mean sharing my life with my family and knowing that my work is contributing to the spiritual well-being of my faith community. To an artist, happiness may come with self-expression and the achievement of public recognition. To a farmer, it may take the shape of a mild winter and good rain for his crops. A mother may find her source of happiness in raising healthy and loving children. Achieving happiness might not be the hardest part, actually finding out what it is that makes us happy is more of a challenge. Trying to define happiness is a slippery task, since happiness means something different to each one of us. But there is a commonality in the fact that we all seem to pursue it. We seek happiness as an end in itself. Unfortunately we often find that when we reach our goal, happiness still eludes us. Furthermore, the concept of happiness evolves for each individual at different points in their lives. If we painted happiness as children it would make a different picture than the same exercise as an adult. Our experiences and social context shape our perception of what being happy means.

The dictionary defines happiness as a state of well-being and contentment; a pleasurable or satisfying experience. But why is there a need to define happiness? Wouldn't it suffice to say that it is the ultimate goal that we all live for? Not at all. It is indeed of prime relevance to find out what happiness means for us. Recognizing the nature of happiness may be more pivotal to our ethical behavior than we realize at first. There is the question of whether happiness affects the ethical judgments of individuals. A paper recently published by Prof. Harvey James of the University of Missouri-Columbia contends that it does. Happy people are more likely to be just and ethical than unhappy people. It further suggests that the ethical conduct of individuals can be controlled in part by changing the institutional environment so as to improve the personal well-being or perceived satisfaction of members of society. Hence, instead of confronting the problem of unethical behavior through the enactment and enforcement of laws, societies could improve the ethical behavior of their citizens by directing scarce resources toward educational or social programs that increase quality of life. A provoking theory. If happiness is related to ethical conduct, then "quality of life" factors that improve subjective well-being might also play an important part in reducing corruption worldwide. In our country, the pursuit of happiness is given such relevance that it is recognized in the constitution as an inalienable right of the individual, right up there with life and liberty. Government does not confer happiness, of course, but gives us the opportunity to obtain it for ourselves. And since we know now that happiness goes hand in hand with ethical behavior, it is in our best interest, as a society, to encourage each of us to find happiness. It is our ethical duty to pursue happiness and to aid others in their own pursuit.

How can we determine what makes us happy? One question you may ask yourself is this: if you had twenty-four hours to live, how would you spend them? Would you be talking to your financial advisor or to your lawyer? Maybe. It is conceivable that this might make you happy. I have known stranger things. What is most likely, though, is that you would spend the twenty-four hours doing something you enjoy. Something that is closer to your true nature. Maybe you enjoy sports so you would take your kids to a game and buy them silly hats and hot dogs. Or maybe you enjoy nature and you have always wanted to visit Yellowstone. A great majority of us would chose to spend the day with our family and friends, and make sure that we tell them how much we love them and that nothing is left unsaid. If I could recommend a good way to spend your last day on this earth, I would tell you to go out and do good to others. When you get to your twenty-fifth hour I can guarantee that you will agree with me that it has been time well spent. This is a theoretical exercise of course and we can change our minds as many times as we like. The point of thinking about it is to explore what we can do today to give more meaning to our lives so that when our last day comes, it will find us ready. We spend every waking moment building ourselves and adding experiences to our collection of memories. Let us not iconize happiness with symbols imposed by advertising. That would be a waste of a perfectly good opportunity. Let us find out for ourselves what is the dream that we wish to pursue, and then let us pursue it with abandon. My years of experience as a pastor have led me to this knowledge: I can confidently say to you that the road to happiness is best traveled by being true to ourselves and our values.

So what about joy then? Is it basically the same thing? There is an essential distinction between the two. From our discussion on happiness we can observe that it is something that is very distinctly outside of ourselves. Something that we need to "pursue" or "attain". It is an objective, a goal, that lives externally and independently from our own spirit. When we reach this goal, or attain this "happiness" we can tell because of the way we feel. We feel happy. Joy, in contrast, is a state of the soul. The best definition of joy I know was not written in words but in music. When we listen to Beethoven's Ninth symphony "Ode to Joy" we can't help but let our spirit soar to meet the music at the very apex of our soul. Beethoven was known to have a difficult temperament. He had lost his hearing - the one faculty that was of utmost importance to his art. He did not have a happy family life, and he was alternatively revered and reviled by his fans. He was not the picture of happiness, by any measure. And yet this masterful music overcame all these obstacles and flowed from him to reach unparalleled excellence.

Paul speaks of joy as one of the fruits of the spirit (Galatians 5:22). Joy. It is not something we feel, but something we are. Joy is within us all the time, it does not need to be pursued or attained. It only needs to be allowed to **be**. It resides within every human being. It flows from the inside, out. It is permanent, unmoving, unchanging. It is the same when we are children and it follows us all the way to the end of our lives. Being happy is something we experience; being joyful is something we are. So where does joy come from? Where does this joy originate? Jesus answers this questions for us, it comes from the Holy Spirit.

At that time Jesus, full of joy through the Holy Spirit, said, "I praise you, Father, Lord of heaven and earth, because you have hidden these things from the wise and learned, and revealed them to little children. Yes, Father, for this was your good pleasure". (Luke 20:21)

As I work on this chapter, I am experiencing one of the most difficult weeks of my life. It is a paradox that I am writing about joy and happiness as I go through these trials. Although none of what happened can be considered good from a "happiness" point of view, I am encouraged by the words of Psalm 30:5b "*weeping may remain for a night, but rejoicing comes in the morning*." This feeling of woundedness will pass because of the ever-present joy that the Holy Spirit has placed in my heart. When I compare my sufferings to Jesus', they take a different proportion and seem little indeed, since he paid the ultimate price for us. He gave up his life. He gave up his chance at earthly happiness for a much higher reward, eternal joy. "…a joy which is permanent, in contrast to the sorrow which is transient". (John 16:22)

Have you ever wondered what sustains people like the late Mother Teresa? She worked with the poorest of the poor, in the slums of Calcutta. All she saw every day was disease, filth and misery. Yet she walked through it all unscathed, with a quick step and her head held high. She always had a kind word for the sick and the afflicted. We would certainly be hard pressed to find things that could make a person happy in the midst of such extreme human need and deprivation. The source of her joy came from within her, and her faith in Jesus Christ. In an interview Mother Teresa was asked how she coped with the horrible situation she worked in every day, seeing bodies of men, women and children wasting away and dying in her arms. She replied that in the face of each and every one of these people she ministered for, she saw the face of Jesus. That filled her with immense joy, such joy as cannot be described in words. I refer to Mother Teresa as an example because she is a figure we all have heard of. But it doesn't take much to find the same quiet heroes in our hospitals, our schools, our prisons, or our homes for the elderly. Countless men and women go to work every day to serve, to comfort and to heal. They go about their jobs joyfully and spread goodwill along the way. Let us always make sure that we remember them, and that we recognize their gift to us.

On the opposite end of the scale, we observe people that presumably have every reason to be happy. They have wealth, beauty, love, and health. And yet they make an issue of little things, until they ruin their happiness and that of those around them as well. Life certainly has a way of wiping away the smile from our faces. It gets so hard at times. But these ups and downs can only affect our happiness, never our joy. The kingdom of heaven is within us. Any believer who fails to experience joy in the process of living must admit that there is something lacking and search what it is that is missing in his or her relationship with God. I can guarantee that the reason will not likely be a new car or a vacation in the Caribbean. Invariably, the discovery will lead to something within, not without. It may be that the inner-self needs a 'tune-up', much like the experience of Jesus in the Garden of Gethsemane.

Then Jesus went with his disciples to a place called Gethsemane, and he said to them, 'Sit here while I go over there and pray.' He took Peter and the two sons of Zebedee [John and James] along with him, and he began to be sorrowful and troubled. Then he said to them, 'My soul is overwhelmed with sorrow to the point of death. Stay here and keep watch with me.' Going a little farther, he fell with his face to the ground and prayed, 'My Father, if it is possible, may this cup be taken from me. Yet not as I will, but as you will.' Then he returned to his disciples and found them sleeping. 'Could you men not keep watch with me for one hour?' he asked Peter. 'Watch and pray...' He went away a second time and prayed, 'My Father, if it is not possible for this cup to be taken away unless I drink it, may your will be done'. (Mathew 26: 36-42)

'And being in anguish, he prayed more earnestly, and his sweat was like drops of blood falling to the ground.' (Luke 22:4)

We learn that Jesus entered the garden suffering, but came away comforted and strengthened. We cannot seek to replicate the actual experience of Jesus in that instance, as he was preparing to surrender his life for the sake of humanity. We can apply, however, this example to seek a time of introspection and reflection, and pray that God shows us the way to open up the gates to the joy that we have locked up inside ourselves.

When Jesus promises the disciples that their grief will turn to joy, he offers perhaps the most poignant promise of all. "*Until now you have not asked for anything in my name. Ask and you will receive, and your joy will be complete.*" (John 16:24)

Isn't that reason enough to rejoice! His promise to us, is that all we have to do is open our hearts and ask, in His name, in order for the Holy Spirit to fill us with complete joy. In our times of darkness, in our doubts, in our grief. All we need to remember is to find our own Gethsemane, fall to our knees and pray.

BIBLIOGRAPHY

The Holy Bible, New International Version. International Bible Society, 1984.

Aristotle. The Works of Aristotle. Encyclopaedia Britannica, 1990.

Metzger, Bruce Mannin and Coogan, Michael David. The Oxford Companion to the Bible. New York. Oxford University Press, 1993.

ABOUT THE AUTHOR

The life of Dr. Joseph O. Bass has been marked both by great adversity as well as extraordinary achievement. The unexplained death of his father, the subsequent loss of the family farm in Mississippi, and the unwavering faith of his mother - who worked tirelessly to raise her nine children - acquainted the author with the best and worst of the human spirit from an early age.

Dr. Bass overcame ethnic and social barriers to become a pastor, industrial missionary and noted scholar of religion, history and sociology. This remarkable spiritual leader is the founder of the Alpha Baptist Church of Christ, the Alpha Complex – a minority Economic Development Enterprise, the Alpha International Academy of Excellence and the Alpha Ethical Society.

The author's life experiences are described in vivid detail in his powerfully moving biographical work "Without Vengeance", published in 1999, 2002 and 2003.

www.ingramcontent.com/pod-product-compliance
Ingram Content Group UK Ltd.
Pitfield, Milton Keynes, MK11 3LW, UK
UKHW041943190726
13854UKWH00004B/1765